Living with Anxiety

*Daily Tools to Calm Racing Thoughts,
Reduce Overwhelm and Reclaim Inner Peace*

Ripley Chanton®

© 2025 **Ripley Chanton® Publishing. All rights reserved.**

No part of this publication may be reproduced, stored in a retrieval system, or transmitted in any form or by any means—electronic, mechanical, photocopying, recording, or otherwise—without prior written permission of the publisher, except in the case of brief quotations embodied in reviews, articles, or critical works.

This book is a work of non-fiction. It is intended for informational purposes only and is not a substitute for professional medical advice, diagnosis, or treatment. Always seek the guidance of a qualified health provider with any questions regarding a medical condition. Never disregard professional advice or delay seeking it because of something you have read in this book. The author and publisher disclaim any liability arising directly or indirectly from the use or application of any information contained herein.

Ripley Chanton®

Contents

Introduction	7
1. NAMING YOUR ANXIETY, CLAIMING YOUR SPACE	11
Mapping Your Anxiety Landscape—Spotting Your Real Triggers	12
Creating a Personal Safe Space—Your First Grounding Ritual	15
2. THE SCIENCE OF WHY YOU FEEL THIS WAY—WITHOUT THE JARGON	18
What Happens in Your Brain During an Anxiety Spiral	18
Why Your Body Feels Out of Control—And How to Calm It Fast	21
3. CALMING RACING THOUGHTS—NIGHTTIME & BEYOND	25
The Worry Dump: Bedtime Journaling to Quiet Your Mind	25
3-Minute Wind-Downs for Racing Thoughts at Night	28
4. MANAGING PHYSICAL SYMPTOMS IN REAL LIFE	31
The Grocery Store Grounding Script	31
The 60-Second Breathing Reset for Meetings	33
Emergency Calm Kit for On-the-Go Panic	35
5. HANDLING PUBLIC PANIC—TOOLS FOR OUT AND ABOUT	37
What to Do When You Feel a Panic Attack Coming On in Public	37
Navigating Social Events—Scripts for Small Talk Anxiety	40

6. OVERWHELM AT WORK—MICRO-INTERVENTIONS
   FOR BUSY DAYS ... 43
   Pre-Presentation Jitters—A Step-by-Step Reset Plan ... 43
   The Midday "Check-In" for Office Overwhelm ... 46

7. PARENTING WITH ANXIETY—REAL-LIFE
   SOLUTIONS ... 50
   Managing "Mom Guilt" and Anxiety When the Kids
   Are Watching ... 50
   The School Pickup Grounding Technique ... 53

8. BUILDING YOUR COPING TOOLBOX—
   PERSONALIZE, DON'T PRESCRIBE ... 56
   DIY Anxiety Action Plans—Your Fill-in-the-Blank
   Framework ... 56
   "Try This, Not That"—Troubleshooting Popular
   Techniques ... 59

9. TACKLING THE "WHAT IFS"—THOUGHT
   PATTERNS THAT FUEL ANXIETY ... 63
   Breaking the "What If" Cycle—A Guided Reframe ... 63
   The "Worry Window"—Contain Your Anxious
   Thoughts ... 66

10. SELF-TALK MAKEOVER—REWRITING YOUR INNER
    NARRATIVE ... 69
    Spotting the Self-Criticism Loop ... 69
    Rewriting Your Anxiety Story—Gentle Affirmations
    That Work ... 72

11. BOUNDARIES THAT PROTECT YOUR PEACE ... 75
    Saying "No" Without Guilt—Scripts for Friends,
    Family & Work ... 75
    Digital Boundaries—Protecting Your Mind from
    Information Overload ... 79

12. HIGH-FUNCTIONING ANXIETY—WHEN NO ONE
    KNOWS YOU'RE STRUGGLING ... 82
    Managing the Mask—Tools for Private Strugglers ... 82
    The "Invisible Load" Check-In ... 85

13. DECISION FATIGUE—MAKING CHOICES WHEN
    YOU'RE OVERWHELMED 88
    The 3-Step "Good Enough" Decision Formula 88
    Quick Research Box: Why the Anxious Mind Craves
    Certainty 89
    "What Matters Now?"—A Quick Clarity Exercise 91

14. NAVIGATING SETBACKS—STAYING RESILIENT
    WHEN ANXIETY RETURNS 94
    The Reset Ritual—Bouncing Back from Bad Days ... 94
    Progress Over Perfection—Tracking Tiny Wins 96

15. THE POWER OF MICRO-HABITS—BUILDING
    LASTING CHANGE 100
    5-Minute Morning Rituals for Calm 100
    Evening Check-Out—Closing the Day with Self-
    Compassion 103

16. SEEKING HELP—WHEN AND HOW TO REACH OUT . 106
    Is It Time for Therapy?—Red Flags and Green Lights . 106
    How to Find (and Talk to) a Therapist Who Gets It ... 109

17. YOUR SUPPORT NETWORK—ENLISTING ALLIES
    (AND EDUCATING THEM) 112
    The Partner's Guide—Explaining Anxiety to
    Loved Ones 112
    Building Your "Check-In Buddy" System 115

18. HANDLING TRIGGERS—MASTERING YOUR
    ENVIRONMENT 118
    The Trigger Tracker—Spotting Patterns Before They
    Spiral 118
    Real-Life Scenario Playbook—Scripts for Common
    Stressors 120
    The Sunday Prep Ritual—Reducing Weekday
    Anxiety 122

19. PROGRESS YOU CAN SEE—TRACKING,
    CELEBRATING, AND ADJUSTING ... 124
    Anxiety Check-In Logs—Making the Invisible
    Visible ... 124
    Celebrating Small Wins—Turning Progress into
    Motivation ... 126
    When to Adjust Your Toolbox—Signs It's Time for a
    Change ... 128

20. COMMUNITY, COMPASSION, AND YOUR
    NEXT STEP ... 130
    Joining the Conversation—Finding Your Safe
    Community ... 130
    The "Not for Everyone" List—Letting Go of What
    Doesn't Work ... 131
    Your Personalized Coping Toolbox—A Living
    Document ... 132
    The Compassion Contract—A Promise to Yourself ... 132
    Digital Resources—Worksheets, Trackers, and
    Guided Scripts ... 133
    Reader Stories—Real Voices, Real Hope ... 134
    Your Next Small Step—What to Try Today ... 135

    Conclusion ... 137
    References ... 143

Introduction

There's a certain kind of quiet that comes at 2am, when the rest of the house is still and you are the only one awake. Your heart is pounding for no clear reason. Your brain is cycling through what-ifs and should-haves, as if the answers might finally arrive before sunrise. You focus on the ceiling or the soft hum of the fridge, wishing for sleep. You promise yourself tomorrow will be easier, but you know that tomorrow, anxiety might show up again—at the grocery store, in a Zoom call, or while you help your child with homework.

If this scene feels familiar, you are not alone. This book is for you—the person who shows up every day, even when it feels impossible. I wrote this guide for adults who live with anxiety in the middle of real life. I know how heavy it feels to hold it all together. You want relief that actually fits your world, not just another list of tips that work for someone else. You want tools that you can use on the train, in your office, or while standing in the cereal aisle trying to look calm and put-together.

You have probably read other books or tried the advice—deep breaths, positive thinking, maybe even that trendy new app everyone raves about. Maybe you have wondered why the anxiety keeps on finding you. Maybe you feel broken or left behind. You have tried to do everything "right" and still, anxiety lingers. I see the exhaustion, the frustration, the moments when you wonder if anyone else truly gets what it is like to live with a mind that won't settle.

This book is different. Here, you will not find dense chapters full of theory or advice that feels miles away from your daily reality. Each chapter is short. Each tool is practical and grounded in real science. I want you to have micro-interventions you can use in a minute—like a quick script for grounding yourself in the grocery store, or a journal prompt to release worries before bed. There is no toxic positivity here. No shame. No jargon. Only straight talk and real hope.

I wrote this for overwhelmed adults—especially women ages 25 to 55 who carry the weight of parenting, work, studies and caring for others, often while trying to care for themselves. You might be a parent who feels invisible at school pickup, a student frozen by decision fatigue, or a professional holding your breath in every meeting. You crave relief that fits your life, not someone else's ideal. You want a toolbox, not a textbook.

What makes this book unique is that it will focus on your real, immediate needs. I've kept each chapter short and focused. There are quick wins and longer strategies. There are real stories from people who have stood where you stand. You will find customizable tools, fill-in-the-blank action plans, and digital resources you can access on your phone. You can use this book in any order. Jump to the chapter that calls out to you today. Flip to a page when you need a lifeline. This isn't about doing everything perfectly. It's about progress, one step at a time.

I am deeply passionate about helping anxious adults because I have lived this journey myself. I have spent years researching anxiety, supporting clients and testing hundreds of approaches—both as a professional and as a person who has known the sting of panic in the most ordinary moments. I believe in practical change and gentle honesty. I believe that perfection is not the goal. Progress is. Even a small shift can change the shape of your day.

Throughout this book, you'll see real-life vignettes—stories from people who have felt lost in their anxiety and found ways to make life a bit lighter. You'll find action plans you can fill out in minutes. There are maps for tracking your anxiety triggers, bedtime "worry dump" journal pages, and digital tools you can use when you're on the go. You'll learn how to build your own coping toolbox, piece by piece, so you can face anxiety wherever it shows up: at home, at work, in relationships, or while parenting.

You will also find space in these pages for setbacks. Anxiety is not a problem you can solve overnight. There will be good days and hard days. This book gives you permission to start where you are, to take imperfect steps and to try again as many times as you need. You are not alone in this process. You have support here and you can always return to these pages when you need a reminder that progress is possible.

So, here's my invitation to you: Take one next step. Maybe that means reading the first chapter. Maybe it's trying one tool, just for today. Or maybe it's simply allowing yourself to believe that change—real, meaningful change—is possible for you. This is not about fixing yourself. You are not broken. This is about finding relief that works for your life, right now and building a path to inner peace, one small action at a time.

Let's begin.

Chapter 1

Naming Your Anxiety, Claiming Your Space

Last week, I froze over a group text—my chest tight, thumb hovering, convinced a wrong emoji could spark embarrassment. If you've ever had your breath catch for what seems a "small" reason, you're not broken or imagining it. This is anxiety in daily life: creeping in quietly, noticed only when your heart races or your stomach twists.

Naming anxiety is the first step toward reclaiming your physical and emotional space. Many people live with a constant hum of unease, never fully gone. Putting words to these feelings—whether "panic," "dread," or just "overwhelmed"—returns some control. This chapter isn't about badges or labels but about seeing your experience clearly, so you can meet it with understanding, not fear.

People often see anxiety as one overwhelming feeling. In reality, it shows up in familiar patterns—small moments that accumulate and leave you drained. By naming these moments, you'll see anxiety isn't random. For some, it's unread emails or the sound of a school bell, prompting uncomfortable interactions. For others, it might be the clatter of dishes, or relentless chat notifications. These micro-triggers —small sparks—can launch a wave of anxious thoughts or sensations.

Mapping Your Anxiety Landscape—Spotting Your Real Triggers

Pinpointing your triggers requires honesty and curiosity. Give yourself permission to notice what sparks your reactions, even if those sparks seem insignificant. Triggers are more specific than "work" or "stress." They're moments like seeing twenty unread Slack notifications pre-9am, waiting in the school pickup line with lingering worries, hearing your phone's low battery beep during a call, getting a vague "can we talk?" text, or sensing the flicker of overhead lights. They can be as subtle as hunger before lunch, the smell of burnt toast, or a TV show intro tied to past stress.

Common daily micro-triggers include:

- Unread emails climbing higher
- Honking in a carpool lane
- Multiple missed calls from family
- Ambiguous group texts
- Appliances buzzing at night
- Harsh overhead lighting
- Loud nearby chewing
- Skipping breakfast and feeling shaky
- Lingering food scents
- TV shows with stressful themes

To reveal your unique pattern, try a three-day trigger journal:

- Use a notebook or phone to record every spike—a flutter, restlessness, urge to withdraw.
- Log specifics: not just "work stress," but "heart raced after seeing 17 Slack notifications at 8:15 am."

- Even minor triggers matter; writing them down makes hidden patterns clear.

Example Trigger Journal Entries

Day 1 8:15am: Heart pounded after seeing Slack notifications before coffee. 11:30 am: Tight chest entering the break room with coworkers chatting. 3:05 pm: Nauseous waiting for my daughter outside school. 9:45 pm: Restless after watching news highlights.

Day 2 7:10am: Irritable after skipping breakfast—hunger amplifies worry. 1:00 pm: Jaw tense after group text with unclear plans. 5:20 pm: Shaky hands when my phone buzzed during dinner.

Day 3 10:00am: Restless after a leaf blower buzzed outside during work. 2:40 pm: Sad after a sitcom reminded me of college. 7:30 pm: Tired, couldn't settle after checking my bank balance.

Boxed-out list:

Hidden Triggers You Might Overlook

- Certain smells (cleaners, perfume, leftovers)
- Lighting changes (flickering bulbs, dusk)
- Background music or sudden loud sounds
- Time of day (afternoon slump, sunset)
- Hunger or dehydration
- Social media habits
- Specific words or phrases from others

Your anxiety triggers are personal; what sets off one person won't affect another. This isn't about being "too sensitive" or inadequate. Triggers reflect your past, your physical state, even small details from yesterday. There's no right or wrong—just what's true for you.

Three contrasting vignettes illustrate this. Sarah, a parent, dreads the school bell, knowing it means facing other parents and teachers. Jake, a student, feels his heart pounding every time a professor calls on someone—the possibility alone keeps him tense. Priya, who manages a team, finds anxiety surging not in meetings, but right after, replaying her words and worrying she sounded insecure. None of these triggers are silly or shameful—they're just how anxiety knits itself into daily routines.

After three days of journaling, scan for repeating themes. Are weekday mornings tough? Are certain people or places recurring anxiety sources? Create an anxiety map by color-coding recurring triggers or using an app (see resource link in appendix). Draw lines between related moments, noticing clusters—from tech notifications, meal times, or locations. Mood tracking apps or printable charts (like those at PositivePsychology.com) can help visualize these patterns. The goal: Make the invisible visible so you can respond, not just react.

Watch for early warning signs that anxiety is building—physical (jaw clenching, shallow breath), emotional (irritability, dread), or behavioural (doomscrolling, avoiding tasks). Use this quick midday checklist:

- Jaw tightness or teeth grinding
- Shoulder or neck stiffness
- Restlessness or fidgeting
- Urge to withdraw from conversations
- Repeatedly checking your phone
- Irritability over small things
- Feeling spaced out or disconnected

Set a phone alarm for a short midday pause. Even thirty seconds helps you catch these signs before anxiety escalates. Keep tracking and mapping for a week—seeing the patterns laid out often brings unexpected clarity and relief.

Creating a Personal Safe Space—Your First Grounding Ritual

Emotional safety is often overlooked—until it's missing. When anxiety spikes, finding calm can feel as elusive as quiet at a crowded concert. Recall the last time you felt truly at ease—maybe wrapped in a favourite blanket, singing in the car, or simply hearing your own breath with notifications silenced. Emotional safety isn't just about being physically alone or away from chaos; it's the deeper sense of existing unguarded and without the threat of judgment or new demands. This safe feeling is unique: for some, it's when the house is silent after bedtime; for others, it's the rhythmic activity of cooking with music in the background; for parents, the private solace when car doors close; for students, the hush of a library or the isolation of headphones; for professionals, early mornings before the day's rush. Emotional safety shifts with circumstances, but the crucial part is recognizing it for yourself.

Take a moment to ask: "When do I feel most safe, calm, or grounded?" Pause and jot down any moments that come to mind. These don't have to be dramatic—perhaps it's morning sunlight on your face, the routine of nighttime face-washing, or your pet snuggling nearby. Use this answer as your anchor.

Physical space helps with grounding, but you don't need a designated room or elaborate setup to create a safe refuge. Even in busy environments, you can carve out a small, intentional spot just for yourself—a "mini safe space" you can return to, even for sixty seconds. At home, it could be a basket with a soft scarf, calming lotion, and a favourite book or playlist. At work, a drawer stash: a smooth stone, earplugs, or a cherished photo. In your car, keep a small kit: lavender balm, sunglasses, or a stress-relief playlist. The aim: anchor your senses in comfort and familiarity.

For inspiration, consider:

- A work drawer holding scented hand cream, noise-cancelling earbuds and a stress ball.
- A bedside basket with a favourite candle, cozy socks and a journal for late-night thoughts.
- A car console with peppermint gum, tissues and sunglasses to buffer the world.

Customize these kits to your preferences. If scents aren't appealing, focus on texture—something soft or smooth to touch. If music grounds you, assemble playlists for different moods: gentle for anxiety, upbeat for low energy. Don't overlook digital safe spaces—calming backgrounds or guided breathing apps can be instant anchors.

With safety cues in place, it's time to build your first grounding ritual. Rituals help your mind and body slow down and reset. A simple and powerful starting point is the "5-4-3-2-1" grounding exercise, which you can use quietly in any setting—from chaotic work meetings to anxious waits at the pharmacy.

How it works:
Notice five things you can see—the pen on your desk, your mug, a painting, your hands.
Notice four things you can feel—the texture of your jeans, the coolness of the table, moving air, warmth of your breath.
Notice three things you can hear—traffic, hum of electronics, birds, your heartbeat.
Notice two things you can smell—brewing coffee, laundry detergent; if nothing stands out, recall a favourite scent.
Notice one thing you can taste—a sip of tea, or just the inside of your mouth.

This ritual draws your attention away from spinning thoughts and back to the here and now. Use it before meetings, after stressful calls, or while waiting anywhere.

It's normal for grounding rituals to feel awkward or artificial at first—especially if you're worried about others noticing, or if anxiety is already high. With time, they get easier and become small acts of self-care. One reader told me, "At first, I felt ridiculous doing this at work—like everyone could see my hands shaking—but over time, it became my reset button. Now nobody even notices those few seconds." If you get interrupted, just pick up where you left off. If self-consciousness creeps in, remind yourself these moments are for you alone.

If you struggle to focus or get distracted, use an object from your safe space kit—a scent, a texture, or a comforting sound—to help center your attention. Remember: these rituals are flexible. They can and should evolve as your needs shift.

You deserve moments where anxiety loosens and comfort returns, even briefly. Grounding rituals aren't about perfection, but about weaving small moments of relief into your life. With practice, these tools become second nature—quick and private escapes from overwhelm.

Take a deep breath and give yourself permission to create these tiny sanctuaries, wherever you are. Inner calm grows through small, daily acts of care—crafted and protected by you.

Chapter 2

The Science of Why You Feel This Way—Without the Jargon

What Happens in Your Brain During an Anxiety Spiral

Imagine you're sitting at the kitchen table, scrolling through your emails, when suddenly a message pops up from your boss with "Please see me" in the subject line. Instantly, your stomach drops. Maybe you feel hot, your mind starts racing and a flood of what-ifs crowd your thoughts. This is the moment your brain's internal smoke alarm kicks in—sometimes loud, sometimes blaring, even when there's only a little toast burning in the toaster. Your body reacts as if there's a fire, even when all you have is a little smoke.

Your brain has its own built-in alarm system designed to keep you safe. Picture the amygdala as your brain's smoke detector. It's small and almond-shaped, tucked deep inside your head, and its job is to sense danger. The amygdala doesn't bother to check if the threat is real or just a little kitchen mishap—it sounds the alarm just in case. This response helped our ancestors survive real dangers, like wild animals or natural disasters. Today, though, that same system can make your heart race over a calendar invite or an unfamiliar phone number.

A home smoke detector sometimes goes off just because you burnt a piece of toast or took a steamy shower. In the same way, your amygdala can mistake harmless triggers—like a tense conversation or a noisy commute—for real threats. When this happens, it signals to your whole body: "Alert! Something is wrong!" Your thinking becomes focused on what could go wrong and it's almost impossible to concentrate on anything else.

Visual Sidebar:

Home Smoke Detector Amygdala (Brain's Alarm) alerts you to fire; alerts you to danger. Sometimes triggered by steam or toast. Sometimes triggered by stress or uncertainty. Can be helpful—but gets annoying when too sensitive. Can be helpful—but causes anxiety when too sensitive.

The amygdala doesn't work alone. There's another part of your brain —the prefrontal cortex—that acts as your calm-down coach. This region helps you put things in perspective, solve problems and decide what's truly dangerous. When everything is calm, your prefrontal cortex keeps the amygdala in check, sort of like an older sibling reminding the little one that not every creak in the house means monsters are hiding under the bed.

During an anxiety spiral, though, the amygdala gets so loud it drowns out the rational voice of your prefrontal cortex. Imagine you're driving and someone cuts you off in traffic. Your inner alarm blares: "Danger! Something bad could happen!" Before you know it, your thoughts tumble—what if I get into an accident? What if I'm late for work? What if something worse happens? That alarm system is trying to protect you, but it's become too sensitive, blaring at every possible hint of harm.

This tug-of-war between alarm and calm happens automatically. You aren't "choosing" to be anxious or overreact. Your brain is simply wired to notice potential threats first and ask questions later. For many years, I thought my anxiety meant I was just too sensitive or dramatic. But learning how my brain works changed everything for me—and for so many others I know. It isn't weakness; it's your brain doing its best to protect you, even if it gets a little overzealous sometimes (Source 1; Source 2).

Sometimes people blame themselves for spiralling, thinking they should "just get over it" or "stop worrying so much." If this sounds familiar, know that you are not making this up. Your brain is doing its job, only with an alarm that's set a little too loud or too early. There's nothing broken about you. It helps to picture anxiety as something happening in your brain—not something wrong with your character.

Validation Box:

You're not making this up—your brain is protecting you, just a little too much.

If you want to help your prefrontal cortex regain control during an anxiety spiral, one of the fastest ways is to nudge your focus back into the present moment. Here's a quick method: Name three things you can see right now. It sounds simple, but this tiny act pulls energy from the alarm center back toward the logical part of your mind.

Say you're stuck in traffic and feel panic rising. Try this: Look around and name three objects—maybe a blue car beside you, a street sign ahead and the coffee cup on your dashboard. Speaking them out loud helps even more. "Red light, white truck, green tree." This shifts your attention away from runaway thoughts and gives your calm-down coach a chance to speak up.

You can use this technique anywhere—at work after a tough email, at home when the noise feels overwhelming, or even in line at the store when impatience bubbles up. Each time you name what's around you, you build a small bridge from panic to perspective. Your thoughts start to settle; your breath slows down; you remember that you're safe right now.

With practice, these small steps help retrain your alarm system—turning down the volume so it doesn't hijack every moment. Every time you pause to notice what's real around you, your prefrontal cortex gets stronger at talking back to the alarm bells.

Reflection Section:

When was the last time you felt blindsided by anxiety? Take sixty seconds now and recall what set off your alarm. Write down three things you saw in that moment—big or small. Notice how focusing on details shifts how you feel.

Understanding how your brain responds during anxious moments gives you power—not power over every twist and turn of life, but power over how you respond when alarms sound inside your mind.

Why Your Body Feels Out of Control—And How to Calm It Fast

Anxiety doesn't just affect your thoughts—it affects your body in ways that can feel unsettling. Imagine you're about to give a work presentation: your heart pounds, palms sweat, stomach flips, maybe you feel lightheaded or shaky. If these moments make you fear something is wrong with your health, you're far from alone. These physical symptoms come from your body's "fight, flight, or freeze" response, a leftover survival mechanism. When your mind senses a threat—real or imagined—it tells your body to get ready for action. While this once meant surviving physical dangers, now it tends to happen during work meetings or social situations.

Here's what's happening: as anxiety hits, your body instantly reacts. Your heart rate jumps to move more blood to your muscles in case you need to escape. Breathing turns shallow, leaving you dizzy. Sweat beads to keep you cool, muscles tense—even if you're just sitting there. You may feel tingling, chest tightness, butterflies, or nausea. These intense sensations aren't dangerous; they're just your body's way of trying to help.

What your body thinks and what's actually happening; "There's danger! Get ready to fight or run!". You're stressed or anxious—not in true danger. Heart pounds to pump blood. No real emergency—just a work meeting. Muscles tense for quick movement. You're still, but body's on alert. Sweat cools the body. No need to run—body overreacts.

These symptoms often show up when something matters: a job interview, a disagreement, or even just enduring a crowded, noisy store. Sometimes, anxiety strikes without warning and you feel dizzy or sick. Perhaps you've feared a racing heart meant serious illness; often, it's just adrenaline. One reader shared how realizing this was anxiety —not a heart issue—helped her feel less afraid. Recognizing what's really happening can ease the fear these sensations bring.

Tingling, shakiness, flushed skin—these aren't signals of illness, just a hypersensitive threat system. It's like a car engine revving at a red light; the system is running, but the car isn't moving. Your body is cautious and sometimes mistakes stress for real danger.

Common Anxiety Symptoms

You're definitely not the only one experiencing these. Here are the most common physical anxiety symptoms:

- Racing heart
- Sweaty palms
- Shaky hands or legs
- Tight chest
- Stomach aches or queasiness
- Dizziness
- Tingling or numbness

- Tense shoulders or jaw
- Dry mouth
- Hot flashes or chills

Recognizing these as routine responses can make them less frightening. Your body is harmlessly reacting as if it needs to protect you—even if all you have to do is answer a phone call or pick up groceries.

Calming Your Body Quickly

The good news is that you can help your body settle down—often in just a few minutes. A simple and effective tool is called box breathing. It slows everything and sends a calm signal to your nervous system. To do it: inhale through your nose for a count of four, hold for four, exhale gently through your mouth for four, and hold again for four. Imagine drawing a box with each step—up one side as you inhale, hold across the top, down the other as you exhale and hold across the bottom.

4-4-4-4 Box Breathing Guide:

1. Breathe in (count 1-2-3-4)
2. Hold (count 1-2-3-4)
3. Breathe out (count 1-2-3-4)
4. Hold (count 1-2-3-4)

You can use box breathing in any anxious moment: Before a meeting, when you wake up, in traffic. You don't need any special tools—just your breath and focus.

What if Breathing Techniques Make Me Feel Worse?

If slowing your breath makes you dizzy or more anxious (which happens for some), try grounding instead: grab something cold, touch a textured object, move gently, or focus on one sense (like notice five sounds you hear nearby). There's no universally "right" centering technique—experiment to find what works for you.

Understanding and Accepting Your Body's Response

Knowing why your body reacts this way makes these symptoms much less scary. Remind yourself these feelings are normal and temporary, however intense they seem. With practice, tools like box breathing or grounding get easier and more effective at helping you through anxiety.

As this chapter draws to a close, remember: Anxiety can make your body feel out of control, but these reactions are normal and manageable. Each step toward understanding what's happening and practicing calming techniques helps build trust in your own resilience. Next, we'll cover practical ways to calm racing thoughts and handle mental overwhelm when anxiety tries to take over your mind as well as your body.

Chapter 3

Calming Racing Thoughts— Nighttime & Beyond

The Worry Dump: Bedtime Journaling to Quiet Your Mind

There's a strange phenomenon that occurs right after bedtime. The day is finally over—kids are asleep, emails are silenced and your routine is done. For a moment, you hope your brain will quiet too. Instead, your thoughts accelerate: What if I forget that call? Did I say the wrong thing? Why was I short with my partner? The minutes drag as you become tangled in worries and unfinished to-dos.

You're not the only one whose brain races at night. Many anxious adults find their minds hold off until bedtime to review every stray concern. It's like your mind stores unresolved thoughts for just this moment of hoped-for rest. That's where the "Worry Dump" can help. Instead of letting worries churn all night, you give them a home—on paper or in your phone. This process is about release, not solving problems. You're letting your mind know it can rest. Research shows that externalizing your thoughts before bed can reduce rumination, calm your nervous system, and help you fall asleep (see [SOURCE 1]).

Setting up a worry dump is simple. Keep a basic notebook or journal by your bed—one you don't mind scribbling in. Many people prefer using their phone's notes app if handwriting feels slow or if they share a room. Accessibility matters; you want it nearby as soon as your thoughts rev up.

When ready, set a timer for three to five minutes. The goal isn't to craft an essay or make sense of every thought. Write whatever comes to mind, no matter how big, small, random, or repetitive. Don't worry about structure or spelling. This is a true "dump"—every tiny concern, nagging doubt, or lingering fear. For example: "Worried I'll forget the morning meeting. Did I sound weird in the text to Sarah? What if the car makes that noise tomorrow?" Dumping these onto paper helps break the mental loop, making it less likely that they will disrupt your sleep.

If you like more structure, divide your page into two columns. On the left, jot each worry exactly as it comes. On the right, mark it as "actionable" or "out of my control." For example:

- "Worried I'll forget groceries" → Actionable
- "What if my boss thinks I'm incompetent?" → Out of my control
- This approach clarifies what needs true attention and what doesn't, reducing anxiety's hold. You may even realize that most worries can be left for another time.

Sample Journal Entry

Worried I'll forget the morning meeting—should I set another alarm? Did I mess up the numbers on today's report? What if my manager is disappointed? Still thinking about what I said to Sarah—did it come off weird? Need to schedule my son's appointment; worried I'll forget again. What if the car won't start tomorrow? Did I lock the back door? Wish I could just fall asleep.

Remember, the purpose isn't to fix any problem right now. It's to remind your mind: "These worries have been heard but don't have to control my night." Many people worry that writing down fears will make them worse, but most find the opposite—putting them on paper adds distance and quiets the noise. As one reader shared, "I thought seeing my worries listed would overwhelm me, but after dumping them, my brain finally let go for a while."

You don't have to solve anything tonight—just write, then close the book.

Once you've finished your worry dump, and even if the list feels scattered, close the ritual with intention. Use a simple mantra or phrase: "I'll return to this tomorrow if needed. For now, I can rest." Physically closing your notebook or putting your phone face down reinforces this mental boundary. Sleep doesn't have to wait until everything is resolved; your brain knows these worries are safely contained until morning.

If you still fear forgetting something important, add a very short "reminder" list for the next day—just key tasks (e.g., "Set alarm," "Pack lunch," "Email Sarah"). Once they're noted, let them wait until morning.

If writing feels awkward, try a voice memo worry dump. Record yourself naming each worry as if leaving a voicemail: "Okay, brain, here's what's on my mind..." Speaking worries aloud can be just as soothing and gets them out of your head without pen and paper.

Interactive Element: Worry Dump Template

Here's a simple template for your nightly worry dump:

Worry/Thought: Can I Act On This? (Yes/No) Notes/First Step (if Yes) Forgot to send work email; Yes. Add reminder for morning.

What if friend is upset? No. Can check in tomorrow. Will car break down? No. Not in my control tonight

Try filling in one row each night before bed.

Normalizing discomfort is important in this ritual. Facing your worries doesn't mean they'll disappear—but they'll hold less power to keep you awake. You're reminding yourself that it's okay not to fix everything right now. It's enough to acknowledge your thoughts and set them aside until morning.

3-Minute Wind-Downs for Racing Thoughts at Night

You're in bed, the lights are off, but your mind won't slow down. Instead of trying to force relaxation, try these quick wind-downs designed to ease nighttime anxiety without much time or effort. Contrary to popular belief, you don't need a long bedtime routine; even three minutes can help. Here are three micro-rituals that actually work.

First, try the "Gratitude Reset." Get comfortable—lying down or sitting up—close your eyes or soften your gaze. Silently name three things from today that brought comfort, relief, or joy. They can be small—maybe a good cup of coffee, your kid making you laugh, or soothing rain on the window. Don't pressure yourself to feel grateful; just acknowledge these moments. If saying them feels odd, whisper or jot them in your phone's notes app, or use a sticky note on your nightstand as a cue: "Three things." For an internal script: "Tonight I'll notice small things that went okay. My brain can rest knowing not everything was hard." Over time, this gentle shift can move your focus from worries to something softer.

Next is the "Body Scan Calm-Down." Start at your toes and move slowly up to your head. For each part of your body, ask: Is it tense or relaxed? Can I loosen it, even a little? The goal isn't total relaxation—

just notice and soften where possible. If distracted, simply start again with your feet or hands. Breathe gently throughout. If you like, add a calming playlist or white noise app to help signal your brain that it's time to wind down. A note on your pillow or phone charger—"Scan and soften"—can help remind you. This brief check-in grounds you in your body and interrupts anxious thoughts.

The third is "5-4-3-2-1 Senses Downshift." Lying in bed, mentally list: five things you can hear (fridge hum, cars, your breath), four things you can feel (blanket, pillow, air), three things you see (shadows, clock), two things you smell (soap, laundry), and one thing you taste (maybe toothpaste). This pulls your focus to the present moment. You can do this silently, whisper it, or type it into your phone.

Consistency is more important than perfection. Pick one ritual that feels doable and commit to it for a week. Don't worry about skipping a night or feeling awkward at first. Some people use a simple tracker—like a piece of paper by the bed—to check off each night, or an app if you prefer. As one reader shared, starting with just three minutes led to falling asleep faster, but it took a few nights of consistency to notice real results.

Make these routines your own. If gratitude lists aren't for you, recall favourite moments or times you felt calm, even briefly. Pair a body scan with putting on lotion or sitting on the bed before getting under the covers. If you share a room, do a silent or text version. Visual cues help too—like a sticky note or specific pillowcase—as reminders.

Barriers are common when adopting new routines. Maybe you fall asleep while settling your child, or are late after a long shift—tie your wind-down to something you always do, like brushing your teeth or checking your alarm. If three minutes feels too long, try just one and build up.

Feeling awkward or silly is normal at first. Remind yourself that this isn't about perfection—it's about finding what helps your mind shift toward calm and away from chaos. Even imperfect attempts disrupt anxious patterns, building a new connection between bedtime and relaxation.

Troubleshooting Table: Common Wind-Down Barriers & Solutions

Obstacle: Creative Fix "I always forget." Place a sticky note on pillow or set a recurring phone reminder. "No privacy at night." Do body scan quietly while sharing a bed; use mental list. "I'm exhausted already." Pair with brushing teeth or after turning off lights. "It feels awkward." Whisper instead of speaking out loud; type in notes app. "Kids interrupt me." Try wind-down after kids' bedtime routine; include them if possible. "I fall asleep before I try." Do wind-down as soon as you get into bed—even before getting cozy.

Integrating these quick routines into habits you already have makes them easier to remember and sustain.

As you try these this week, notice any effects on your sleep or mood in the morning. Track what works and tweak as needed—make it fit your life. Racing thoughts likely won't vanish instantly, but each wind-down sends your mind the message: it's time to slow down.

In short: easing nighttime anxiety doesn't need to be complex or lengthy. Just a few minutes of a calming ritual can reset your mind and help you prepare for better rest. Next, we'll explore handling daytime anxiety—especially the physical symptoms that can feel urgent and overwhelming.

Chapter 4

Managing Physical Symptoms in Real Life

The Grocery Store Grounding Script

Picture yourself stepping into a busy grocery store, hoping to grab a few items. The aisles are crowded, carts squeak and bright lights seem to pierce your head. As you reach for cereal, your chest tightens and your hands tremble on the cart. Suddenly, thoughts race—What if I faint? Will people notice? How will I get out? The store is a common anxiety trigger: noisy, unpredictable and full of people. You are not alone in this.

Here's a simple grounding script you can use right there, even if you feel like fleeing. First, pause where you are. Rest your hands on the cart handle and take a slow, deep breath. Silently remind yourself: "I am safe. I am in a normal place. I can pause here." These words, even in your mind, can anchor you in reality.

Next, focus on your senses and the physical world. Notice the cool, smooth cart handle against your palms. Look at the bright blue cereal boxes, shiny red apples and green-yellow sale signs. Listen for the refrigerator hum, scanner beeps and a faint intercom announcement.

Each sense you engage acts as a tiny anchor, pulling you away from panic and grounding you in the present.

If you need to move, do it mindfully. Feel the cart handle or run your fingers along a box. Pick up a can and notice its weight and shape. Press your feet firmly into the floor and wiggle your toes. These subtle movements help you stay connected to your body and keep your attention away from anxious thoughts. None of this is about looking calm for others—it's about stabilizing yourself.

You may think everyone's watching, but the reality is people are lost in their own shopping routines. One reader was certain her shaky hands would draw attention near the freezer, but nobody noticed. "I was convinced I looked ridiculous," she shared, "but honestly, nobody noticed." Lean on your cart or step aside if you need to; most people are too focused on themselves to notice.

Boxed Tip

You're allowed to pause, lean on your cart, or step to the side—most people are too busy to notice.

If your anxiety becomes overwhelming, allow yourself to step away. Find a quieter aisle or head to the restroom for a few calming breaths. There's no shame in taking a moment for yourself—it helps prevent anxiety from getting worse. If you have a support person, text them: "Struggling in the store—just pausing." Just knowing someone knows can help reduce the feeling of isolation.

Practice this grounding script during calmer, low-pressure shopping trips. Take short visits during off-peak hours and ground yourself while waiting in line or bagging groceries. Each success—however small—builds confidence, like climbing a "confidence ladder." Start by walking through the produce section, or checking out at self-checkout. Over time, add more: wait in longer lines, shop during busier times, chat briefly with a cashier. Every small win helps retrain your mind and body to handle anxiety in real-world situations.

Eventually, these tools become second nature—the feel of the cart handle, the sound of beeping scanners, the press of your shoes on the floor—all reminders that you are safe and capable in spaces that once felt overwhelming.

The 60-Second Breathing Reset for Meetings

Meetings can feel like a stage where you have to keep it together, even when your heart pounds or your skin prickles with sweat. The room fills with chatter and shuffling papers, yet you notice your hands start to tremble. You want to look focused, but inside, a current of anxiety threatens to sweep you away. This is when the "4-2-6" breath becomes a secret lifeline—a simple, nearly invisible way to anchor yourself. Here's how it works: inhale softly through your nose for four seconds, hold your breath for two and exhale slowly through your mouth for six. Let the exhale draw out longer than the inhale, coaxing the nervous system toward calm. You can repeat this rhythm two or three times, adjusting the speed if needed. Tell yourself quietly, "No one knows I'm doing this—my breath is my anchor." This phrase acts as a shield, reminding you that even in a crowded room, you have control over your internal landscape.

Blending this breathing reset with subtle movements helps reinforce its effect. Under the table, press your thumb and index finger together gently, syncing each squeeze with the exhale. The sensation sharpens your focus and gives you a tactile cue to follow the breath's flow. Another quiet trick: ground both feet flat on the floor and picture roots growing downward, spreading through your shoes into the earth below. The image isn't just a distraction; it's a stability cue, telling your body you're steady right here. If you feel tension rising in your legs, try pressing your knees gently together or placing your palms flat on your thighs, fingers relaxed. These choices are invisible to others but signal safety to your nervous system.

Physical symptoms often flare in meetings—shaky fingers, clammy palms, or sudden warmth crawling up your neck. Instead of fighting these sensations or judging yourself, respond with a quick self-compassion script. Think: "This feeling will pass; I am steady enough." If possible, keep a cool drink within reach or stash a small stress ball in your bag or pocket. Touching something cool or textured gives your body a point of focus outside the anxiety spiral. If you're worried about sweaty hands during a handshake or while taking notes, dab them with a tissue under the table or rest them on your lap until the sensation fades.

Preparation helps take the edge off meeting anxiety before it spikes. Rehearse the 4-2-6 breathing technique while on a solo call or during quiet work periods. The more you practice in safe settings, the more automatic it becomes in stressful ones. Make it part of your pre-meeting ritual: before logging into Zoom or stepping into a boardroom, take a minute to run through one cycle of the breath and grounding movement. One reader told me she started practicing during virtual meetings where her camera was off, noticing her thoughts slow and her body loosen. By the time she entered her first in-person staff meeting, the technique felt familiar—she reported feeling more present and less hijacked by panic.

If you struggle with intrusive thoughts—worries about stammering, blanking out, or being judged—pair the breath with a mental reminder: "People are focused on themselves, not my symptoms." This isn't about tricking yourself into confidence but gently shifting attention away from your body's alarms. Over time, every small success rewires your response to anxiety triggers in these settings.

The beauty of this reset is its portability and discretion. No special tools required, no need for anyone to notice. You can deploy it in high-stakes presentations or casual team huddles alike. It's yours—an internal anchor you can return to again and again, no matter what's happening around you.

Emergency Calm Kit for On-the-Go Panic

There's a reassuring sense in knowing that, wherever you are—be it stuck in traffic, on a noisy train, or waiting at a doctor's office—you can reach for something that helps you steady yourself. That's the purpose of an emergency calm kit: a pouch or zip lock bag you fill with a few small, sensory items. This isn't about having every technique at your fingertips, just a few grounding objects you like and will actually use. Practical ideas include a favourite scented hand lotion, a couple of mints or gum, a smooth stone or textured keychain, a calming playlist on your phone and a small notepad with encouraging affirmations. It doesn't need to be elaborate—three to five items that feel personal and comforting are all you need. For example, some people use a simple pencil case, filling it with lavender lotion, peppermint gum, a worry stone, earbuds and a slip of paper reminding them, "This moment will pass." The point is not to have everything, but to carry something that reassures you when you most need it.

When you sense panic building—your heart racing, palms sweaty, mind unmoored—your calm kit serves as your anchor. Even if your hands shake, open it. Run through your senses. Squeeze the stone, feel its texture. Spread scented lotion on your wrists and breathe in slowly, letting the scent ground you. Pop a mint for a burst of flavour. Listen to your playlist or calming sounds with your earbuds. For sight, focus on something nearby—your notebook's colour, a pattern on your scarf, the laces on your shoes—and really notice the details. Use the "5-Senses Countdown" as a guide: five things you see, four things you feel, three things you hear, two things you smell, and one thing you taste. Each sensation helps return your attention to the present moment.

This kit isn't about weakness or hiding. It's genuine self-care—just like bringing a water bottle or snacks for a long day. If you ever think, "I should be able to handle this without props," remember, having tools ready is preparation, not failure. Update your kit with the seasons or as your needs and tastes change—swap in a warmer scarf for winter, or update your music if something new soothes you more.

Sometimes you'll forget your kit at home or in your car. That's normal. To avoid being caught off guard, stash a backup mint tin in your desk, a spare worry stone in your coat pocket, or another pouch in your glovebox. If you worry about others noticing, use a makeup bag, sunglasses case, or pencil pouch—most people won't pay much attention and will just assume you're organizing or freshening up.

Some days, the kit might not be enough—and that's okay. Just knowing you have it can ease anxiety before it arises. On especially rough days, remember to give yourself credit for seeking support instead of just enduring the discomfort alone.

In short, anxiety doesn't have to control everything. Carrying an emergency calm kit is a way of preparing and caring for yourself before panic sets in.

Visual: Sample Calm Kit

A small zippered pouch might include:

- Lavender hand lotion
- Peppermint mints
- Smooth river stone
- Wired earbuds
- Mini notepad with affirmations

Physical symptoms may always be part of anxiety, but they don't have to dominate your life. With simple tools like grounding scripts, breathing resets and calm kits, you have real ways to steady yourself anywhere. Over time, these strategies add up, giving you back some control even when life feels unpredictable. Next up: building a personalized coping toolbox that fits your daily needs.

Chapter 5

Handling Public Panic—Tools for Out and About

What to Do When You Feel a Panic Attack Coming On in Public

You're standing in line at the pharmacy, trying to focus on your phone, when a wave of dread tightens your lungs and reddens your neck. The room feels too bright and sounds are too sharp—you worry everyone can see your panic. The urge to escape is overwhelming, but life goes on around you. Whether in a school lot, at your desk, or on a crowded train, you've likely faced this: racing thoughts, clammy hands, the instinct to run or freeze. You are not alone, nor are you weak for needing help in these everyday moments.

When panic strikes in public, you need quick, subtle tools. That's where the "Panic Protocol"—Pause, Anchor, Plan—comes in. Designed for places you can't escape, it lets you get relief without drawing attention, whether in a carpool line, at a post office, or squeezed into a concert crowd.

The first step: **Pause**. Just stop for a moment—tell yourself, "I can spare ten seconds." Feel your feet on the floor. If you can, touch something cool—a railing, wall, or your wrist. This interrupts racing thoughts and reassures your nervous system that you're safe.

Anchor is next. Reconnect with your body and your environment in discreet, small ways: try three slow exhales while staring at your shoes or hands, making your exhale longer than your inhale to signal your brain that danger has passed. Silently count down: three breaths, two thumb taps, one shoulder roll. If keeping still is difficult, shift your weight gently or squeeze an object—a keychain, stone, or your sleeve. These grounding methods are quick, barely visible to others, but can help you regain control (see source 1 in APA list).

Last: **Plan**. Decide what you need next, without shame. Scan for a "safe spot"—maybe a bathroom stall, a bench, or just the exit. If you can't leave, visualize a protective bubble around yourself, separating you from chaos. Standing near a window, finding a quieter aisle, or moving closer to the door also helps. If you have an emergency kit item—a familiar scent or a grounding object—use it now to remind yourself of safety.

Environmental cues can powerfully soothe. Train yourself to identify "rescue zones"—a quiet library corner, a back auditorium row, or your car with your favourite playlist. When panic rises, remind yourself that small havens exist everywhere if you plan ahead. Mentally map out safe spots in places you frequent: a calm restroom, a low-traffic bench, or a shady spot outside.

Worrying about what others might think if you step away is common. Remember: you don't owe anyone an explanation for taking care of yourself. Simple, direct statements work: "Excuse me, I just need a moment," or "I'm going to step outside for some air." Most people will leave it at that. If someone insists, add: "I'm not feeling well, but I'll be back soon." You're not being rude—just protecting your well-being and boundaries (see source 4 in APA list).

If you feel guilty for leaving—maybe you left a dinner early or skipped a lunch—pause and ask whose comfort matters most right now. Once, I left my friend's party after twenty minutes when panic overwhelmed me. At first, I worried she'd be upset. Later, I realized putting my health first was right and any good friend would want me safe over silently suffering.

Tiny Victories: Celebrate What Counts

- Stayed ten minutes longer than last time at a crowded event
- Finished checkout despite panic
- Stepped outside for air before things worsened
- Texted a friend for support
- Left early without apologizing or over-explaining
- Used a grounding object discreetly

Every small win is progress—not about "beating" anxiety, but reclaiming parts of your life from it.

Notice when and where panic flares up. Keep brief notes after these moments: Where were you? What helped? What could you try next time? Over weeks and months, this log becomes your personal blueprint, improving your responses (see source 2 in APA list).

Panic in public is more common than you think—manageable, survivable, nothing to be ashamed of. Pausing your day or leaving early is not failure; it's courage. Some days, getting through checkout is a major victory; other days, just parking outside the building counts as success. Your progress is real, even if unseen.

Remember: You're allowed to protect your peace anywhere—at work, at school events, in crowded places or quiet waiting rooms. Panic grows when hidden in shame; every time you use these tools, you reclaim a bit more freedom.

Navigating Social Events – Scripts for Small Talk Anxiety

Picture yourself getting ready for a networking mixer, neighbourhood party, or your child's PTA meeting. You check your outfit, practice a smile and wonder if others feel just as awkward. Maybe you scroll your phone for conversation ideas, but it seems like everyone else is prepared with stories and confidence, while you just hope to get through without turning red or forgetting someone's name. Events like these can feel overwhelming, where every laugh or silence feels magnified. Social anxiety thrives in these settings, feeding on fear of awkward silences, being judged for stumbling over your words, or forgetting introductions.

It's common to feel nervous walking into a crowded room. The buzz of conversation, clink of glasses and people grouping up quickly can trigger old fears. Your mind may replay past slips or convince you everyone else has it easy. But discomfort during small talk is normal—something many experience, no matter how composed they may seem. Readers have shared stories of planning every word before an event, only to go blank when asked, "So, what do you do?" One mother even described sitting in her car outside a reception for fifteen minutes, trying to muster the courage to go in, terrified of standing alone.

Social gatherings have unique triggers. Some people dread being asked about their weekend and drawing a blank; others worry about mispronouncing a name or forgetting something from a previous chat. Some feel anxious about being drawn into groups that seem more connected and for some, even making eye contact or waiting in line for food feels like a test. If you find yourself rehearsing lines while brushing your teeth or riding the elevator, you're not alone.

Preparation helps ease anxiety. Having simple, ready-to-use small talk scripts can bridge awkward pauses and keep you anchored when your thoughts freeze. Here are a few fill-in-the-blank lines that suit almost any setting:

- "I'm so glad we both made it here—how did your week go?"
- "I'm always a little nervous at events like this—do you come to these often?"
- "Excuse me, I'm going to grab a drink—would you like anything?"
- "I'm trying to meet a few new people tonight—mind if I join you?"

Don't feel forced to use them word-for-word. Adjust them to match your style or situation. The goal is to have something rehearsed for support when anxiety strikes.

Your body language matters as much as your words. You might find yourself crossing your arms, fidgeting, or staring at your phone. Instead, try standing with relaxed shoulders and visible hands—maybe holding a drink, snack plate, or your keys. Practice occasional soft eye contact, even if it feels unnatural at first. If it helps, position yourself near an exit or window for comfort—a subtle assurance that you have an escape route. These small actions signal openness and help calm your nerves.

Holding an object—your phone (on silent), a favourite bracelet, or just a cup—can ground you physically, redirecting anxious energy into something tangible. When a conversation overwhelms, quiet agreement ("mm-hmm," "oh wow," "that's interesting") can buy you time before speaking.

Sometimes anxiety peaks and you need an excuse to step away without drawing attention. Here are some gentle exit lines for almost any situation:

- "I need to check in with someone—be right back."
- "Excuse me, I have to make a quick call."

- "I promised myself I'd say hello to someone else tonight—I'll catch up later."
- "I need some air—I'll see you in a bit."

Practice these exits ahead of time so they feel natural. You don't have to explain further and most people won't press for details. Plus, the classic bathroom break is always a safe option.

Taking breaks during events is healthy self-advocacy, not a sign of failing at socializing. You don't need to apologize for stepping out or leaving early if it brings you relief. The pressure to stay until the end is real, but your comfort is more important.

Navigating social gatherings with anxiety isn't about becoming the life of the party or forcing yourself into endless conversations. It's about showing up on your terms: prepared with scripts, supported by intentional body language and permission to leave if needed. The more often you practice—even trying one new line per event—the more confident and less drained you'll feel with time.

As this chapter ends, remember: Social anxiety doesn't define your ability to connect with others. With preparation and permission to set boundaries, these events become more manageable. Next, we'll look at handling overwhelm at work, where deadlines and expectations add another layer to anxiety, but can be managed with practical tools like these.

Chapter 6

Overwhelm at Work—Micro-Interventions for Busy Days

Pre-Presentation Jitters—A Step-by-Step Reset Plan

You're just outside the conference room, slides ready, sleeves pulled taut across nervous hands, waiting for your name on the agenda. Your mouth is dry. Maybe your heart's pounding, hands slightly trembling and you wonder if it's noticeable when you click that first slide. Suddenly, notes blur and your mind is like a crowded subway—noisy and unfocused. This is the anxiety that comes with presenting, speaking in meetings, or fielding questions at work. Even the seemingly confident feel exposed at times.

You're not alone in these anxious moments—many people stare at the clock, waiting for their turn. The workplace is full of triggers: a sudden request to "say a few words," tech glitches, slide malfunctions, or surprise questions from unfamiliar or intimidating colleagues. The fear of being judged or making a mistake heightens the pressure, making even seasoned professionals feel vulnerable.

One reader, Maya, shared: "My heart races and my mind goes blank before I speak—even if I've practiced for days. I feel like everyone can tell how nervous I am." Her story is common. Performance anxiety doesn't mean you're unprepared or unsuited for leadership—it means you care and want to do well.

This is where a rapid prep ritual helps. When nerves build, it's tempting to battle or suppress them. But what if you viewed that energy as readiness? Like an athlete before a race, your body's not shutting down; it's gearing up, preparing you to focus and respond. That surge of adrenaline can sharpen your senses. If you view nerves as fuel, the whole experience shifts.

Here's a three-minute reset you can do before your turn—be it for a presentation, meeting, or group sharing.

Step away briefly if possible—to the hallway or restroom. Take a deep breath and plant your feet on the ground. Relax your shoulders, unclench your jaw, let your arms hang. For thirty seconds, name what you're feeling: "This is anxiety. My heart is racing. My hands are cold." Research shows labelling emotions can calm the brain and restore clarity (see Source 1).

Now, focus on breathing: inhale through your nose for four counts, hold for two, exhale slowly through your mouth for six. Repeat two or three times, keeping the exhale longer than the inhale. This signals your system that it's safe and slows your heart rate (see Source 1). For something tactile, press your thumb into your palm or touch a cool object—a pen, ring, or even cold water.

Next, ground yourself using your senses. Name three things you see—maybe a carpet pattern, clock, or someone's shirt colour. Listen for two sounds—the hum of air, distant voices. Notice one thing you physically feel—your feet in your shoes or the air's temperature. This anchors you in the present and eases anxious spirals.

Before speaking, reframe nerves as care about what you share. A colleague once joked, "What if I let myself be imperfect today? What's the worst that will happen—forgetting a line?". Treating mistakes with curiosity—"How will I handle this?"—helped her ease up on perfectionism.

Another reader, Tracy, realized nerves meant she cared and was ready to give her best. Turning anxiety from a threat into a sign of engagement can be transformative.

After presenting—regardless of how it went—pause before racing back to normal duties. Don't dissect every detail or replay possible flubs. Take a decompression moment: Stand if sitting, stretch your arms overhead, or walk to shake off leftover adrenaline.

Do a quick "Success Scan." Silently note one thing that went well ("I answered that tough question calmly" or "I kept talking even while nervous") and one thing to improve next time ("Next time, bigger notes" or "Ask for clarification if tech fails"). This isn't about perfection—just growth, breaking the self-criticism loop after stressful events.

Finish with a self-compassion mantra: "I did enough. I am enough." It may feel odd, but regular practice helps quiet the inner critic (see Source 3). If needed, drink some water or step outside before resuming your day.

Interactive Element: Workplace Reset Checklist

Keep these steps handy:

- Name your emotion: "This is anxiety; I feel nervous."
- Breathe: 4-count inhale, 2-count hold, 6-count exhale—repeat three times.
- Ground: Name three things you see, two sounds you hear, one thing you feel.
- Reframe: Nerves = readiness.

- Humor/Curiosity: "What if I let myself be imperfect today?"
- Success Scan: One win, one lesson.
- Mantra: "I did enough. I am enough."
- Movement: Walk/stretch/drink water.

With use, these rituals become second nature. Each time you use them—whether addressing a crowd or a small group—you prove to yourself that anxiety can visit, but it doesn't get to decide what happens next.

The Midday "Check-In" for Office Overwhelm

Workdays often feel like a conveyor belt. You move from one task to another, powering through emails, jumping on calls and trying to keep up with everyone's requests. By lunchtime—or honestly, by 10 a.m.—your brain might already be spinning. Sometimes you realize you haven't taken a real breath since you sat down, or your shoulders are up by your ears and you can't remember the last time you blinked away from the screen. One reader told me, "I was powering through emails but realized I hadn't breathed deeply all morning." The truth is, overwhelm rarely announces itself with fanfare. It sneaks in quietly, stacking up in your mind and body until the smallest thing—an unexpected email or a printer jam—tips you over the edge. That's why I rely on the midday "check-in," a tool that acts like a circuit breaker for mounting anxiety and decision fatigue.

A check-in isn't just another break. It's a deliberate pause for self-awareness—a two-to-five minute window where you actually notice what's happening inside you, not just around you. Think of it as pressing pause on autopilot. You're not scrolling your phone or chatting with a coworker; you're giving yourself space to notice your mental, emotional and physical state before the stress avalanche rolls any further.

Here's how to turn this idea into something real and useful. Start by settling in your chair or stepping into a quiet spot if you can. Take a few slow breaths and ask yourself three basic questions: How am I feeling mentally? What emotions are floating around? What is my body saying right now? This is the "Scan & Soothe" method—a structured self-check script that can reveal what you need most in the moment. Maybe your mind is foggy or frazzled, maybe you feel impatient or discouraged, or perhaps your body aches from hours at the keyboard. Jot down quick answers on a sticky note or in your notes app—no need to be poetic or thorough, just honest.

For example:
Mind: "Scattered, distracted."
Emotions: "Frustrated, anxious."
Body: "Tense neck, shallow breaths."

Noticing patterns over time can help, too. Maybe every Wednesday at 2pm, you're always cranky and foggy after back-to-back meetings. When you spot these patterns, you can plan for them—maybe taking a micro-break right before that usual slump.

Once you've checked in, the next step is to interrupt the overwhelm with an ultra-brief reset. You don't need fancy equipment or a yoga mat—just sixty seconds and some intention. My go-to is thirty seconds of box breathing: inhale for four counts, hold for four, exhale for four, hold again for four. Repeat twice. This simple breathwork slows your heart rate and sends a "calm down" message through your whole system. If breathing exercises aren't your thing or make you dizzy, try the "Window Break." Stand up and look out the window—even if it just faces a parking lot or a patch of sky. Let your eyes wander for one minute. This gives your brain something neutral to focus on and breaks the mental loop of worry.

Another favourite is the "Desk Reset." Pick one small area—maybe a cluttered corner or your pen cup—and tidy it for sixty seconds. This isn't about Marie Kondo-ing your entire office; it's about moving your body and giving your mind a sense of completion. Organizing something physical, even briefly, can create a surprising sense of control and order when everything else feels chaotic.

To make this ritual stick, build in reminders that work for your schedule and style. Calendar alerts work well if you live by Outlook or Google Calendar—set one at the same time every day, maybe after lunch or before a big meeting rush. A silent phone alarm can also nudge you without disturbing anyone else. Some people go old-school with a sticky note on their monitor ("Check-in?") or keep a small object—a smooth stone or bright paperclip—on their desk as a visual cue to pause.

One reader shared, "My 2pm alarm reminds me to breathe and now my whole afternoon feels lighter." It's not magic; it's just creating space for relief before stress hardens into anxiety.

Sometimes check-ins get skipped—maybe the day runs away from you, or you forget entirely until bedtime. That's normal. Any check-in, even once a week, is progress toward more mindful days. If guilt sneaks in about missing one, remind yourself that this tool exists to help you, not judge you.

This isn't another item on an endless to-do list; it's a kindness to yourself in the middle of chaos. With repetition, these pauses become part of your work language—a way of protecting your energy and sanity when everything else feels out of control.

The more often you show up for yourself in these small ways, the more resilient you'll feel when stresses pile up. Even one intentional pause can shift the tone of your afternoon or help you catch burnout before it takes over. Micro-interventions aren't about fixing everything—they're about giving yourself room to breathe and reset before anxiety takes center stage.

As this chapter closes, remember: Overwhelm at work doesn't mean you have to power through until breaking point. With small but regular check-ins and resets, you gain back moments of calm and clarity, even on the busiest days. These habits are stepping stones toward deeper peace and better boundaries—tools that will carry forward as we look at managing anxiety in parenting and family life next.

Chapter 7

Parenting with Anxiety—Real-Life Solutions

Managing "Mom Guilt" and Anxiety When the Kids Are Watching

Trying to hold yourself together for your children while dealing with anxiety is a unique challenge. Everyday moments—shaking hands while making breakfast, losing patience during sibling fights, or snapping too loudly—can trigger intense guilt. Later, you replay these moments, haunted by fears: "Am I screwing them up? Will my anxiety hurt them?" This blend of self-doubt, quiet perseverance and persistent "mom guilt" shapes parenting with anxiety. As one reader shared, "I worry I'm not a good enough parent when my anxiety flares in front of my kids." If that sounds familiar, you're not alone.

Guilt appears unexpectedly: snapping at your child over a mess, cancelling playdates because you need quiet, or letting TV run longer so you can breathe. It might be craving alone time, worrying your child notices your anxiety, or feeling like a failure for needing to step away. These feelings are amplified by the fear of judgment from teachers, family, or other parents who might seem to be silently assessing you.

Quick Fact Box:

Anxiety is not a parenting failure—most kids benefit from seeing adults manage tough emotions. Children learn emotional literacy by watching how adults handle difficult moments, not by seeing constant calm (see APA list: 27).

It's natural to want to protect your children from struggle, but pretending anxiety doesn't exist doesn't shield them. In reality, it can make feelings seem scarier and harder to talk about. Instead, acknowledge your feelings with honest, age-appropriate words—it helps your child find language and confidence for their own emotions. This doesn't mean unloading your worries on them, but rather modelling that feelings are okay and showing healthy ways to cope.

For toddlers and young kids, keep it simple: "Mommy feels a little nervous right now. I need to take some deep breaths." For school-age kids, add: "Sometimes grown-ups feel worried too. I'm going to sit and calm down." Teens can handle more: "I've been feeling anxious today. It's not your fault. I'm taking care of it by using some things that help me." Always reassure them it's not about them and that you're managing it (see APA list: 32).

Naming your own anxiety out loud validates emotions as normal and teaches kids that feelings pass and don't need to be hidden. For example: "I'm having a tough moment, but I know it will pass." This simple act lets children talk about their feelings without shame.

When anxiety spikes around your kids, self-compassion is essential. You might only have seconds to regroup. The "Hand on Heart" technique can help: place your hand over your chest, close your eyes if possible and take three slow breaths. Remind yourself, "I am allowed to feel anxious. Parenting is hard and I'm doing my best." Even with your kids nearby, these two minutes can soften anxiety and keep you grounded (see APA list: 3).

If you need to excuse yourself briefly, even a two-minute break can help reset your mood. One mom used to say, "I need to use the bathroom," then take a short pause to breathe while tiny fingers tapped outside the door. This isn't selfish—it's survival. Sometimes, invite your child to co-regulate: "I'm feeling wound up. Let's take a deep breath together." Hugging your child while breathing slowly calms both of you and models self-soothing during stress.

The fear of parenting judgment is real. You might picture other parents whispering or teachers silently evaluating your parenting. Even relatives can add pressure with endless patience or unwanted advice. But your worth as a parent is defined by care and effort, not by how calm or perfect you look. Presence, not perfection, matters most.

Vulnerability can also lead to support. One reader found comfort after sharing her anxiety in an online parent group. She posted after a hard week and was met with dozens of replies from other parents who felt the same way. Sometimes, being honest invites community.

If you need support, try: Connecting with a friend who understands, joining an online mental health or parenting group (where honesty is valued), or seeking out a school counsellor or mental health professional (many schools offer resources for families facing stress and emotional challenges; see APA list: 23).

Interactive Element: Self-Compassion Pause Exercise

Take one minute. Place your hand on your heart or chest, close your eyes or soften your gaze. Breathe in slowly for four counts, hold for one, and exhale for five counts—repeat three times. Silently say: "I am doing my best in this moment. It's okay to need help. I am not alone." Notice any shift in tension, even a slight one.

Parenting with anxiety isn't a failure. It's an opportunity to show your kids resilience, self-compassion and honest communication. When you're open, kind to yourself and seek support when needed, you give your children tools they'll use for life—even on messy, imperfect days.

The School Pickup Grounding Technique

School pickup brings its own brand of anxiety—an odd blend of hurry, waiting and invisible pressure. You're probably juggling a mental checklist as you inch along in the car line or scan the sidewalk for familiar faces. Maybe your heart starts thumping every time you spot the cluster of parents chatting by the entrance, or you feel a wave of dread when you realize you forgot to sign another permission slip. The transition from your own day into "parent mode" is rarely seamless. Pickup can be a minefield: traffic jams that make you late, last-minute reminders about missing homework, or that one parent who always catches you with small talk when you're hoping to avoid conversation altogether. There's also the unpredictable stress of sudden schedule changes—an email announcing early dismissal, or overhearing a bit of gossip about after-school activities. Each of these micro-triggers can pile up until the simple act of picking up your child becomes a source of tension.

It's not just about being there on time. For many, waiting in the car or standing on the curb brings a restless energy. You might find yourself fidgeting, scanning your phone repeatedly, or rehearsing what you'll say if someone approaches. One parent described, "My heart races in the pickup line, especially on days when I have to talk to other parents or teachers." Maybe you're wrestling with the urge to avoid eye contact, or calculating how quickly you can make a polite exit. The pressure to appear calm and collected, while inside you're counting down the minutes until you can retreat, is real.

To make these moments easier, it helps to have a quick, private grounding technique you can use right in the car or as you wait on foot. I call this the "Anchor in the Car" method. If you're seated, start by planting both feet flat on the floor mat—press down gently and wiggle your toes. Feel the texture beneath your shoes. This simple physical action reminds your body that you're supported and safe, even when your mind is buzzing. Let your hands rest on your thighs or grip the steering wheel; notice their temperature and weight. Take a slow inhale through your nose for four counts, hold for one and exhale through your mouth for six. Repeat this breath cycle three times. With each exhale, picture tension draining out of your body and into the floor. If you're walking to meet your child, focus on the sensation of each step—heel, toe—and match your breath to your pace: inhale for two steps, exhale for three. This rhythmic movement and mindful breathing can help anchor you, even in a crowd.

Handling surprise interactions with other parents or teachers takes a little preparation too. You don't need an elaborate plan—just a few ready-made scripts that help you move through social encounters without extra stress. For those days when you don't have energy for more than a nod, try the simple "smile and wave" approach: a quick smile, a small wave and a friendly "Hi! Busy day, huh?" This lets you acknowledge others without inviting a long conversation. If someone tries to draw you into an extended chat and you feel anxiety rising, use a gentle exit line: "Good to see you—I have to run to another errand, but let's catch up soon." Practicing these lines out loud at home—even just once in front of the mirror—can make them flow more naturally when you're feeling tense.

Carrying a small comfort object can also make a difference. Tuck a smooth stone, piece of fabric, or favourite hand lotion in your bag or pocket. When nerves spike, squeeze or touch your chosen item while breathing slowly. The sensory cue grounds you in something familiar and reminds you that support is literally within reach.

Once pickup is over, both you and your child might be carrying leftover stress from the day. Building a post-pickup transition ritual can help everyone reset before diving into homework or evening routines.

One idea is creating a "transition playlist" for the ride home—choose one calming or happy song that signals it's time to shift gears. Play it every day if possible; over time, it becomes an audio cue for relaxation. If music isn't your thing, try "snack and chat" at home: sit together with a favourite snack and share one "rose" (best part) and one "thorn" (hardest part) from the day. This practice encourages honest conversation while keeping things light.

Physical movement works wonders too. Invite your child to join in a mini "shake it out" session—put on music or set a two-minute timer and take turns shaking arms, legs, or even doing silly dances before homework starts. This playful ritual helps release tension for both of you, making the next part of the day feel less overwhelming.

Dealing with paperwork or school announcements often adds another layer of stress. Rather than tackling all forms in isolation or rushing through them during dinner prep, turn them into a shared moment if possible. Read school updates together at the kitchen table or sofa, turning an obligation into connection. You might even make it visual with coloured pens or stickers—anything that reduces dread and makes routine tasks feel like less of a burden.

School pickup doesn't have to be just another anxiety trap in your week. With small grounding habits, simple social scripts and post-pickup rituals, you can transform these stressful minutes into opportunities for calm connection—with yourself and your kids.

When you look back on these afternoons, try to notice not just what went wrong but also where things felt smoother than before. Remember: Progress is rarely dramatic; it often hides in these little shifts and rituals tucked between errands and car doors closing. In the next chapter, we'll dig deeper into building your own coping toolbox—so you always have support at hand, no matter where anxiety shows up next.

Chapter 8

Building Your Coping Toolbox— Personalize, Don't Prescribe

DIY Anxiety Action Plans—Your Fill-in-the-Blank Framework

Think of building your coping toolbox for anxiety like picking out your own tools from a hardware store—some old, some new, all suited to your style. This isn't about following a set manual, but about creating supports that genuinely work for you. No two toolboxes are the same, because no two people experience anxiety the same way. That's not just okay—it's essential.

Many people get discouraged by "one-size-fits-all" solutions. Some find meditation apps life-changing, while others, like me, can't sit still and prefer moving or cleaning to shake off anxiety. You may have noticed that other people's solutions don't always fit. That's because anxiety is personal—your triggers, energy and comfort objects are unique to you. Personalization isn't extra—it's crucial for these tools to work (see APA list: 25).

The best part of building your own coping toolbox is that it evolves with you. Some days, all your "fast calm" tricks will come in handy;

other days, you might need to refresh your favourites when they grow stale. Your toolbox isn't fixed—use it at home, at work, out with friends, or in tough parenting moments. It doesn't even have to be physical. You might keep notes on your phone, sticky reminders, or just have mental checklists at the ready.

Let's create your action plan step by step. Grab a notebook, open a notes app, or print the worksheet at the end of this section. Start by listing:

- **My Top 3 Fast-Calm Tools:** Quick resets—box breathing, a stress ball or stepping outside for a minute or two.
- **Tools for Public Anxiety:** What helps when you're out —maybe a grounding phrase ("I'm safe here"), fidget jewellery or a water bottle.
- **My Go-To Self-Compassion Rituals:** How do you show yourself kindness? Try a hand over your heart, a gentle phrase ("I'm doing my best") or a soothing song.
- **People I Can Text or Call:** Write down two or three people who "get it" and won't try to fix you when you reach out.
- **Grounding Reminders that Work for Me:** These help you return to the moment—touching cool surfaces, naming five things you see or using a scent like citrus oil from your bag.

You might want to organize or photograph your physical toolbox (maybe a pouch in your bag or a drawer at work), or keep it all digital —do whichever is easiest for you.

Interactive Element: Sample Coping Toolbox Template Download or Print:

[Scan QR code or visit www.livingwithanxietybook.com/toolbox]

A sample filled-out template:

Section: My Tools. Top 3 Fast-Calm Tools; 4-2-6 breath, cooling lotion, step outside. Tools for Public Anxiety; Fidget ring, grounding phrase: "This will pass," texting Jen. Go-To Self-Compassion Rituals; Hand on heart, listen to "Weightless" track. People I Can Text/Call; Jen, Mom, therapist. Grounding Reminders; Name 3 colours in the room, squeeze stone.

Keep this document where you'll see it, either printed somewhere private or as a quick-access note.

Now, picture different scenarios—how might your tools shift based on your setting? At home, maybe it's deep breathing or five minutes of journaling. At work, maybe it's desk stretching or using a sticky note with positive self-talk ("I can handle one thing at a time"). In social settings, it could be holding a cold drink or focusing on one conversation. At night, try a worry-dump journal or white noise. With kids around, your toolbox might simply be stepping into another room for a minute or inviting them to "shake out" tension together.

It helps to keep "backup" tools for days when nothing seems to work. Your favourites may lose effectiveness sometimes—that's normal, not failure. For example, if breathing exercises make you dizzy, try moving instead—a brisk walk or a few jumping jacks. If calling a friend feels like too much, text or write your feelings down, then delete them.

Review your action plan regularly. Set a monthly reminder to see what's still working or what isn't. For example, if "walking outside" isn't doable in winter, maybe switch to indoor yoga or guided visualization. Celebrate these shifts—they show how you're growing. As one reader shared, "What helped six months ago isn't helping now—time to swap tools." That's not backsliding; that's adaptation.

Give yourself permission to outgrow strategies guilt-free. Update your toolbox as often as you want. If you discover something new—sound therapy or art—give it a try. The goal isn't perfection, but steady progress and flexibility.

Above all, honour every small improvement as real progress. Even replacing one tool deserves celebration. If you like tracking, use stickers on a calendar or a mood-tracking app (see APA list: 5). Your toolbox is yours—a growing collection that offers support whenever you need it and reminds you that you're never without help.

"Try This, Not That"—Troubleshooting Popular Techniques

If you've ever felt frustrated by anxiety advice that just doesn't fit, you're not alone. It can feel like the world is shouting solutions—meditate, journal, breathe deeply, repeat affirmations—but some of these tools can actually make things worse for certain people. Maybe you've been told to use a gratitude journal, only to find your brain rebels at the thought of finding three "good" things each day. Or perhaps a well-meaning friend swears by meditation apps, but you can't sit still without your thoughts racing even faster. It's easy to blame yourself when a popular tip backfires, but here's the truth: It isn't your fault if a strategy doesn't click. Your brain and body have their own way of responding and not every technique will suit your chemistry or situation.

Let's get real about some of these tools. Meditation apps are everywhere, but for some, sitting in silence only amplifies the noise inside. A reader once told me she'd tried guided meditation every night for a month and ended up more anxious, not less. Gratitude journals can feel forced or hollow when you're struggling just to make it through the day. Deep breathing, especially in the middle of a panic spike, sometimes makes you lightheaded or even more on edge. Affirmations—those cheerful-sounding mantras—can ring false or even spark self-criticism when you're not in a good place. Mindfulness colouring books might leave you feeling restless or bored rather than calm. The world pushes these options as universal solutions, but they're not one-size-fits-all.

It helps to spot when a technique isn't working and pivot instead of pushing through misery. If deep breathing makes you dizzy or your chest tighter, try grounding through movement: stand, stretch, walk to another room, or even shake out your hands. If meditation feels impossible, swap it for a creative outlet—drawing, cleaning, or cooking while paying attention to the sensations and sounds (see APA list: 3). If gratitude lists feel like chores, switch to a "worry dump" before bed or jot down neutral observations instead ("It rained today," "I ate breakfast"). For affirmations that trigger a wave of negative self-talk, experiment with self-compassion scripts: "It's okay to feel this way," or "I'm learning to be kind to myself." Mindfulness colouring not your thing? Try listening closely to music, or focus on tactile grounding with a textured object.

Here's a troubleshooting chart you can use as a quick reference:

If you feel...During...Try this instead: If you feel dizzy during anxious, deep breathing; try movement instead—walk/stretch/shake out. If you feel more restless or anxious during meditation; try mindful chores—washing dishes/folding laundry. If you feel frustrated, disconnected during gratitude journals; try worry dumps or neutral observations. If you feel triggered or sad, during affirmations; try gentle self-compassion scripts. If you feel bored, annoyed during colouring books, try music or tactile grounding (fidget).

Sometimes a tool that's wildly helpful to someone else is just going to irritate you—or make your anxiety worse. That's normal. It doesn't mean you're broken or resistant; it means you need something different. I've spoken with people who felt enormous pressure to "just meditate" because everyone else seemed to love it. One woman admitted she dreaded her daily gratitude list but kept going because she thought she "should" feel better by now. Eventually she dropped it and felt relieved—that guilt and pressure lessened once she gave herself permission to stop trying what wasn't working.

I encourage you to experiment with new techniques but also keep track of what genuinely feels helpful versus what drains you. Create two lists—a "Try List" for things that go well and a "Not-For-Me List" for those that don't. Use a simple chart in your journal or an app-friendly version on your phone. Track over a week: What did you try? How did it actually feel? Write down surprises—maybe movement soothed you while affirmations did not. If you work with a therapist or support group, sharing your "Not-For-Me List" can be freeing. It reduces shame and helps others see that there's no universal answer.

A reader once told me, "Letting go of what didn't work was actually a relief." She found her energy for healing grew when she stopped forcing techniques that just weren't for her. There's something powerful in dropping the pressure and trusting your own experience.

Self-compassion is key here. Flexibility is not only allowed; it's vital. You might adore box breathing this season but crave music therapy or walks in cold weather. Both are valid. You aren't failing if you outgrow something—it's a sign you're evolving and listening to what works now. If an old favourite stops working, put it in storage for later and try something fresh. I like to keep an "open slot" in my toolbox—a kind of wild card space for new discoveries, so my support system can grow with me.

As you move forward with your toolbox, remember that the right tools change over time and that's part of growth. Don't let anyone tell you there's only one way to calm anxiety; your path is yours alone.

This flexibility is real strength—being willing to adapt means your toolbox will always serve the person you are now.

In closing, the most important thing is that you keep experimenting with honesty and patience. Let yourself release what doesn't serve you and welcome new possibilities as they arise. This isn't about nailing the perfect routine; it's about finding what helps today. Up next, we'll look at how to create boundaries that protect your peace—and make space for all the progress you're making, one step at a time.

Chapter 9

Tackling the "What Ifs"—Thought Patterns That Fuel Anxiety

Breaking the "What If" Cycle—A Guided Reframe

Imagine sitting at your kitchen table late at night, scrolling through your calendar as tension settles in your shoulders. Your mind races: What if I say something wrong at tomorrow's meeting? What if my child gets sick at school and I can't get there? What if I miss a deadline? Each question spawns another, trapping you in a web of worst-case scenarios that feel as real as the chair you sit on. This isn't just overthinking; it's a cycle where your mind tries to anticipate every possible disaster, even those unlikely to occur.

"What if" spirals are one of anxiety's most common forms. Most people miss them because they blend in with daily worries. Listen for shifts in your self-talk: "What if I mess up?" "What if I forget?" "What if I can't handle this?" Physical signs might appear too—tight chest, clenched jaw, or a sudden urge to check your phone. Sometimes, you're lying awake, replaying future events as if failure is certain. At these times, anxiety becomes a script you replay endlessly.

Recognizing this "what if" cycle is the crucial first step to breaking it. Your mind leans into forecasting, convinced that worrying means you'll be prepared for anything. But in reality, this keeps you trapped in fear, not protected. That's why you need practical tools to interrupt the cycle and anchor yourself in the present.

Here's a step-by-step exercise to reframe anxious spirals. First: Write down the exact "what if" thought the moment you notice it. Use a notebook or notes app—just capture the worry as it appears; for example, "What if I bomb the presentation?" or "What if my child is hurt on the field trip?" This slows your mind and provides space to see the thought as a prediction, not a fact.

Next, ask yourself: "Is this happening right now, or am I predicting the future?" This question pulls you from autopilot into awareness. Most often, you'll realize you're worrying about something that hasn't happened. Grounding yourself in the present weakens anxiety's hold.

Then, balance your feared outcome with a neutral, realistic one. If you think, "What if I say something stupid at the meeting?" add, "I might stumble, but most people won't care." Or, "I might forget a point, but I can check my notes." This isn't forced positivity, just an honest contrast to anxiety's doom.

Finish with this reframe: "Even if [feared event] happens, I can [realistic coping action]." For example, "Even if I blank during my presentation, I can pause and take a breath." Or, "Even if my child calls in sick, I can figure out a way to help." This phrase shifts power away from anxiety, reminding you of your ability to cope.

Anxiety convinces us that bad things are likely and unmanageable. That's why "evidence checks" are so helpful. When anxiety says, "What if this disaster happens?" gently counter: "When have I worried about something like this before? How did it actually turn out?" Recall times you worried about an email or meeting that ended up being fine. Most fears never happen—and when they do, you handle it better than you thought. Maybe you missed a deadline once and fixed it. Maybe you forgot something in a meeting, but no one remembered. Gathering these examples teaches your brain that anxious predictions are rarely reality.

It also helps to have a personal reframe script for anxious moments, such as: "My brain is trying to protect me, but I can't predict the future." Or, "I notice I'm worrying; I can come back to the present." You aren't trying to stop worry entirely, just step off the mental hamster wheel of catastrophizing.

Interactive Element: "What Ifs" Thought Cloud Worksheet

Draw a cloud on paper or use the worksheet (QR code at chapter end). Inside, write every "what if" thought on your mind, big or small. Around the cloud's edge, list a realistic or coping response for each worry. For example:

- What if I mess up at work? → Even if I do, I can ask for help and learn from it.
- What if my friend is upset with me? → Even if so, we can talk about it.
- What if I can't sleep tonight? → Even if sleep is hard, I can rest and try again tomorrow.

Keep this sheet visible or save it on your phone for quick access when anxiety rises.

Catching and reframing "what if" thoughts takes practice and patience. These worries are not a sign of weakness—they show your brain is trying to protect you. The more you question and redirect them, the easier it becomes to return to reality instead of swirling in anxious predictions. Over time, this skill becomes automatic—your new method for handling uncertainty and fear.

The "Worry Window"—Contain Your Anxious Thoughts

Anxiety loves open space. Let it roam and it will fill up your entire day, sneaking into work meetings, dinner prep, or even moments when you're supposed to just be relaxing with a show. I remember a time when I could barely focus at work because my brain kept circling the same worry all day long. It felt never-ending, like there was no off switch. That's the trouble with anxious thinking: it's sticky and persistent and before you know it, you're replaying the same fears while folding laundry or standing in the checkout line. If you've ever wished you could "turn off" worry, you're not alone. The good news is, you can't always stop anxious thoughts from popping up, but you can give them boundaries—this is where the "worry window" comes in.

The "worry window" is a simple technique: You set aside a specific chunk of time each day—maybe ten or twenty minutes—just for worrying. That's right, instead of trying to ignore or banish your thoughts, you give them a scheduled spot, like an appointment on your calendar. Think of it as putting your worries in a box for later, so they don't leak everywhere and take over. You still acknowledge those anxious thoughts, but you don't allow them to boss around the rest of your hours. One reader told me, "I used to lose entire afternoons to the same topic—now that I have a worry window after dinner, I can focus at work again." This is not about suppressing or pretending your fears don't matter; it's about giving them boundaries instead of free rein.

You're not ignoring your worries, just giving them boundaries.

To set up a worry window, start by picking a consistent time and place. Some people choose after dinner when things are winding down. Others prefer a quick walk after dropping off the kids or taking ten quiet minutes before bed. The key is being regular—same time, same spot. That way, your mind learns when it will get space to process its concerns.

Throughout the day, when a worry tries to hijack your attention, grab a sticky note, small notebook, or open your phone's notes app. Jot down whatever comes up—no need to analyze it yet. Then tell yourself (out loud if you want): "I'll think about this during my worry time." It can feel odd at first, especially if you're used to wrestling with thoughts right away. But with repetition, this redirect starts to work. You become the boss of when worry gets center stage.

When your worry window opens, settle in and review your list. This is the time to let your thoughts roam free. Don't censor yourself or try to make your worries logical—just write or think through whatever's on the list. If you want, set a timer for ten or fifteen minutes and let yourself go all in: "Okay brain, what have you got?" Sometimes you'll find yourself spiralling a bit; that's okay. You're giving anxiety its space on your terms.

When your timer goes off or you finish reviewing the list, close things down with a brief calming ritual. This could be closing your notebook with intention, stretching your arms overhead, stepping outside for fresh air, or playing a favourite song for sixty seconds. The ritual tells your mind that worry time is over for now. You're released back into the rest of your day.

Many people feel resistance at first. You might worry that you'll forget something important if you don't handle it immediately. Or maybe it feels weird to schedule worry like an appointment. That's normal. One reader told me, "I was sure I'd miss something big if I waited until my window—but writing my worries down calmed that fear." It's common for new users of this technique to feel awkward or doubt that it will help. Stick with it for a week and see how it shifts things.

FAQ: What if worries pop up outside my window? Redirect them to your list and use a grounding phrase like, "Now isn't the time—I'll come back to this later." You might need to repeat this often at first; repetition is part of making it stick. Over time, you may notice worries lose their urgency by the time your worry slot rolls around.

Tracking can help too. Try keeping a tally of how many times a worry actually feels less pressing by the time you get to your window. Some readers discover that concerns that seemed huge earlier in the day now feel almost silly or less urgent. One woman shared, "Half my list felt pointless by evening—my brain just needed to unload it somewhere safe." These small victories build over time and show that giving worry boundaries really works.

Every minute you limit worry is a win—progress, not perfection.

Celebrate these steps as real progress. The goal isn't erasing anxiety from your life; it's containing its impact so you have more mental space for everything else that matters. Even if only some of your worries shrink before their time slot, that's still progress worth noticing.

In closing this chapter, remember: Anxious thoughts might still visit, but they don't get free access to every part of your life anymore. The "worry window" lets you take back control in small but powerful ways—creating structure where there once was chaos. Next up: We'll look at how these reframing techniques connect with building self-compassion and resilience for whatever tomorrow brings.

Chapter 10

Self-Talk Makeover—Rewriting Your Inner Narrative

Spotting the Self-Criticism Loop

Picture this: You spill coffee before a big meeting, forget an invitation, or fall behind on chores. Suddenly, your inner voice chimes in: "Why can't you just get it together? What's wrong with you?" This self-critical voice is common—especially among adults balancing work, parenting and studies. For many, anxiety manifests as constant self-judgment, sometimes loud, sometimes a quiet whisper, always striking at vulnerability.

Negative self-talk often goes unnoticed. You might think, "I'm so weak. Others handle this better," or "If I were stronger, I'd have figured this out." These aren't just passing thoughts—they're mental patterns that emerge during stress, fatigue, or feelings of overwhelm. Some hear them after work mistakes, others while scrolling social media or looking in the mirror. There's also the classic "This shouldn't be so hard," which only fuels shame when things already feel challenging.

To recognize these patterns, try keeping a "thought log." Use a notebook or a phone app to record harsh thoughts exactly as they appear, without editing. Questions to guide you: What were you doing? What triggered the thought? What words did your mind use? Reviewing these entries over several days will reveal which negative phrases recur during anxious moments.

Interactive Element: Is This My Inner Critic Talking? (Quiz/Worksheet)

- Do you often think, "I'll never get this right" or "I'm such a mess"?
- After something stresses you out, do you replay your mistakes and judge yourself?
- Does a small error make you feel like something is wrong with you?
- Do you compare yourself and always fall short?
- Would you ever talk to a friend the way you talk to yourself?

If you answered yes to even two, your inner critic is likely strong and persistent.

Real-life examples drive this home. Emily, a 29-year-old grad student, says, "Every time I get feedback on my papers, I hear, 'You're not smart enough for this program.' Even positive comments are drowned out by my focus on the critical ones." Jamie, a part-time working parent of two, reports, "One missed school email and I think, 'Bad mom—other parents wouldn't forget.' I even apologize for things that aren't my fault." Alex, a manager under pressure, shares, "If I freeze in a meeting, my mind skips straight to 'You're an imposter. You don't belong.'" Though their stories differ, the pattern is similar: Criticism takes over.

Why does this happen? It's partly due to our brain's "negativity bias"—paying more attention to threats, criticism, or what could go wrong, because this once helped our ancestors survive. Add anxiety, and your brain sees extra "danger," so it adopts tough self-talk as a misguided form of self-preservation: If I spot my mistakes and punish myself, maybe I can avoid repeating them. In reality, this only feeds anxiety, draining confidence and energy (see [SOURCE 2] in APA list).

Think of your mind as an intense coach yelling from the sidelines. It believes criticism will motivate you, but often, it just makes you exhausted and erodes your self-worth. Frequent self-criticism creates habitual phrases—"I always mess up," "Never good enough," "Why bother?"—that quickly fire off under stress and become automatic thought patterns.

Besides emotional harm, this self-criticism loop affects actions. People ruminate for hours over small errors, replaying an awkward comment or worrying about an email. Some avoid risks or challenges, reasoning it's better not to try than to invite more self-blame. Shame builds up, making it harder to ask for help or admit difficulty. As one reader put it, "Beating myself up only made me feel more stuck—never less anxious." Eventually, even simple tasks seem overwhelming.

So, how do you change this narrative? It starts with awareness—becoming a "conscious observer" of your thoughts. Notice when your inner voice shifts from neutral or supportive to harsh and judgmental. Do a self-talk scan: After a difficult moment—a tough conversation, a work setback, or a parenting slip—pause and ask, "What did I just say to myself?" Pay attention to the tone (harsh?), volume (loud, persistent?), repetition (does it loop?) and content (always negative or extreme?). You might realize how critical your own words often are.

Practice helps build awareness. Set phone or calendar reminders: Three times daily, pause for thirty seconds and check your self-talk. At day's end, write down a memorable phrase—positive or negative. Patterns will emerge, revealing triggers that make your inner critic louder.

The goal isn't to eliminate all negative thoughts—that's not realistic—but to notice them before they spiral. With practice, you can catch the self-criticism loop as it starts, giving yourself the chance to choose a different response next time.

Rewriting Your Anxiety Story—Gentle Affirmations That Work

When anxiety peaks and old thought patterns return, it's tempting to rely on advice like "just think positive" or "choose happiness." However, forcing yourself into a relentlessly upbeat mindset rarely works and can worsen how you feel. This is called toxic positivity—pressuring yourself to see only the good, ignoring your real feelings and making you hide your struggles. It can leave you feeling isolated in your very normal experience. Supportive affirmations are fundamentally different: They meet you where you are, allowing honesty and supporting understanding rather than judgment.

Gentle affirmations work because they're believable. Instead of reciting phrases like "I love myself completely" when you barely like yourself, start with what's true. If anxiety tells you, "I'll never get through this," try, "I've survived this feeling before," or "It's okay to feel what I feel right now." These words don't deny your pain; they add kindness and perspective. Another helpful phrase: "I am learning to care for myself." This isn't about demanding perfection—just acknowledging that you're doing your best.

A reader once shared how she changed her harsh inner script. She would think, "I'm a mess," every time she felt overwhelmed, but she tried, "I'm having a hard time and that's okay. That's being human." This shift didn't erase her anxiety, but helped her feel less alone and broken, saying, "It changed everything. I could breathe again."

To build affirmations that work—especially during anxiety spikes—use a fill-in-the-blank approach. Good affirmations are specific, honest and meet your real needs. Try: "Even when I feel ____, I can _____." For example:

- "Even when I feel panicky, I can breathe and wait for it to pass."
- "Even when I feel exhausted, I can rest and give myself a break."
- "Even when I feel overwhelmed at work, I can ask for help or step outside."
- "Even when I feel like hiding, I can text one friend or write out my worries."

Simple language is best—what matters is that your affirmation feels true to you. Recall a recent moment when anxiety hit: What did you wish someone had said? Use your own words if possible; these will be strongest for you.

To create your own gentle affirmations, jot down one or two situations that regularly cause anxiety. Then fill in the template in a way that's honest but hopeful. For example, if parenting triggers self-doubt: "Even when I feel like I'm failing as a parent, I can remember all the ways I try every day." Or, if social situations are difficult: "Even when I feel awkward at this party, I can take one deep breath and remind myself that everyone feels this way sometimes." Keep statements simple—no need for grand promises.

Making affirmations stick takes practice, especially in anxious moments. That's when the "Reframe and Repeat" technique helps. When you catch harsh thoughts ("I always mess this up"), pause and say your gentle affirmation out loud or silently. Repeat it at least three times. Pair it with a physical cue—hand on heart, squeeze your fingers, or take a deep breath. Some readers pair affirmations with a gesture like sipping water. This physical action can help you remember to use your affirmation, even when your mind is racing.

It might feel awkward at first, but that's normal. The goal isn't to convince yourself everything's perfect, but to soften anxiety's sharpest messages.

Integrating Gentle Affirmations

Try using affirmations as morning intentions while brushing your teeth or having coffee: "Today I will be kind to myself." During your commute, repeat an affirmation at red lights or on the train: "I can handle whatever comes my way today." At night, set a reset: "I did enough today; it's okay to rest now." Sharing affirmations with friends or support groups can make them more powerful, as you support each other and remind yourselves that kindness is possible, even on hard days.

If you doubt affirmations work, remember feeling awkward is part of the process. Self-criticism may be your default, so trying something new takes time. Give affirmations a week—notice even small shifts: Maybe you ruminate less, recover from anxious spells faster, or just feel more supported by your own mind.

Over time, these small bits of self-kindness add up. How you talk to yourself changes how you handle anxious moments—and how you handle anxious moments changes your overall story.

Remember: Rewriting your inner narrative isn't about crafting a perfect life or erasing all criticism. It's about offering yourself the same compassion you'd give a friend—especially during struggles. Next, we'll explore boundaries and how they help protect your peace and keep anxiety from taking over.

Chapter 11

Boundaries That Protect Your Peace

Saying "No" Without Guilt—Scripts for Friends, Family & Work

Picture this: You're finally relaxing after a long day when a friend texts, asking you to help her move this weekend. Instantly, you feel tense—you're already stretched thin with work and family obligations. Even so, you reply, "Of course! Just send me the details." Later, resentment builds. You wish you'd said no, but guilt and the fear of disappointing her were louder. You're left exhausted and irritated—mostly with yourself.

If this feels familiar, you are not alone. Setting boundaries is especially challenging for anxious people. Anxiety and people-pleasing often go hand in hand; the urge to keep everyone happy and avoid conflict can outweigh your own needs. For many, saying yes feels safer than admitting you can't do something—you might fear seeming selfish, unreliable, or being labelled "difficult." Conflict can feel unbearable, so you avoid it—even if it costs your well-being. As one reader put it, "I agree to things I don't want to do, then feel resentful and exhausted." That's a common anxiety trap: Guilt and worry make overextending yourself feel easier than facing a moment of discomfort.

Why do we get stuck? Internal blockers abound: Fear of disappointing others, FOMO, worry that people will think you're rude or that you'll face confrontation. Often this people-pleasing is a survival skill learned early on—especially if you grew up in a home where conflict felt unsafe or love was conditional (see source 4 in APA list). Chronic boundary violations, though, fuel more anxiety and resentment (source 1). When you always say yes, obligations pile up, eating away energy for rest or the things you value. If you're simmering with frustration, it's your mind and body warning you—something needs to change.

Crucially, saying no isn't selfish—it's self-care, an investment in your peace and sanity. Setting limits isn't about shutting people out, but about making space for what truly matters. Boundaries aren't rigid walls; they're gentle fences between your responsibilities and others', clarifying your needs and non-negotiables. Protecting them is healthy and essential for managing anxiety.

How do you actually say no without being consumed by guilt or over-explaining? The secret: Keep it kind, clear, and brief. No need for elaborate stories or apologies. Here are some effective scripts:

- "I wish I could, but I'm not available."
- "Thanks for thinking of me, but I have to pass this time."
- "That doesn't work for me right now."
- "I'm at capacity and need to focus on what's already on my plate."
- "I appreciate the invite, but I need some downtime."

Notice how these don't invite debate or negotiation. You don't owe anyone a detailed explanation. If they push back ("Are you sure? Can't you just...?"), calmly repeat: "That doesn't work for me right now." Remind yourself: Your worth isn't determined by your availability.

At work, boundaries can be even tougher to maintain. Maybe your boss drops a project on you last minute, or a coworker asks for yet another favour. The urge to say yes is strong—maybe you fear being seen as unreliable or worry about job security. Nonetheless, the same principles apply: Concise, kind boundaries matter more than detailed excuses.

Try these at work:

- "I'd love to help, but my schedule is full."
- "I need to focus on my current priorities to meet my deadlines."
- "That isn't possible for me right now."

Practice these phrases out loud in private. Repetition helps them feel more natural and accessible when anxiety tries to freeze you.

One powerful way to protect your peace is to set boundaries in advance, not just in the moment. If certain requests repeat—babysitting with little notice, weekend work communications, repeated volunteer asks—create default responses so you're not caught off guard.

Write polite auto-replies for recurring emails: "Thank you for reaching out! I'm focused on existing commitments and am not taking on new projects at this time." For draining texts or DMs: "Hey! I'm laying low this week and might not be very responsive—hope you have a great one." Planning ahead reduces decision fatigue, making it easier to maintain boundaries even during stress.

Before the week begins, write down your non-negotiables—a brief list of things you will and won't do. It might be "No double-booking evenings" or "One social plan per weekend." Reviewing your list when you're feeling pressured grounds you in your values. Practice saying no in low-stakes moments—decline an extra loyalty card or turn down free samples—to build confidence for bigger situations.

Saying no isn't a magic fix for all discomfort. Sometimes, guilt and anxiety stick around after asserting a boundary, even when you know it was the right move. This is where self-compassion is crucial: It's normal to feel uneasy, but discomfort isn't danger. Remind yourself, "It's normal to feel uncomfortable, but discomfort is not danger." Acknowledge how hard it was and recognize your courage.

Interactive Reflection Section: Post-Boundary Self-Care Journal

After you set a boundary—especially a difficult one—pause and reflect:

- What did I gain by saying no?
- How did it feel in my body right after?
- What would I tell a friend who did the same?

Record your thoughts. Reward yourself kindly—a short walk, a favourite treat, or even a congratulatory note to yourself ("Proud of you for protecting your peace today"). As one reader said, "Every time I set a boundary, it gets a little easier." You teach your brain that saying no won't wreck relationships or shut doors—it makes space for what matters.

With consistent and gentle practice, boundaries become a source of freedom: Freedom from resentment, overwhelm and the endless loop of agreeing when you should have said no.

Digital Boundaries—Protecting Your Mind from Information Overload

Your phone is likely always nearby, with notifications lighting up your screen before you finish your morning coffee. News headlines scroll by, group texts buzz and social media feeds flood your mind—sometimes with humour, but often with stress or overwhelm. For those living with anxiety, this endless digital input isn't just inconvenient—it becomes ongoing background tension. As one reader said, "Scrolling before bed makes my mind race and I can't sleep." If your heart has raced after late-night doomscrolling or you've compared yourself to others' highlight reels, you know how technology can hijack your peace.

Digital anxiety triggers are everywhere. Doomscrolling—that habit of endlessly absorbing negative headlines—leaves you feeling low and powerless. After-hours work emails blur the line between work and rest, making relaxation tough. Group texts become digital to-do lists, constantly demanding your attention. Social media comparison spirals can damage self-esteem in seconds. Even a flood of notifications for sales, calendars, or weather can create a sense of chaos. These may seem minor, but they accumulate, feeding anxiety and draining your energy.

This is more than feeling busy. Science shows constant digital stimulation increases stress hormones like cortisol and disrupts your body's natural sleep cycles. Blue light from screens at night tells your brain to stay awake when it should be winding down, leading to trouble falling or staying asleep—especially for those already dealing with anxiety or insomnia. Waking up tired only perpetuates the cycle, driving you back to your phone first thing in the morning.

Before making changes, observe how technology really affects you. Where does your anxiety spike when using devices? Is it checking work emails late, waking up to a pile of unread messages, or getting lost on social media when you meant to relax? Notice what you're doing, how long you spend and how you feel afterwards. This is about building awareness, not judgment.

Now for practical boundaries. You don't need to ditch your phone or wipe every app. Start small and be realistic—try one or two of these:

- **Set "phone curfews"** by turning off non-urgent notifications after a certain time (7 pm works for many).
- **Move social media apps** off your home screen or log out after each use so you pause before scrolling.
- **Use "Do Not Disturb" or Focus Mode** during meals, family time, or before bed.
- **Check email in set blocks**—maybe each morning and afternoon—instead of leaving it open all day.
- **Limit news exposure** to once or twice daily from sources you trust.
- **Mute group chats** temporarily if they're overwhelming.
- **Disable unneeded notifications** that aren't urgent or valuable.
- **Create tech-free zones:** make the dinner table or bedroom screen-free.
- **Charge your phone outside the bedroom** to prevent late-night scrolling.

Communicate Your Boundaries

Setting boundaries with people is just as essential as those with devices. Sometimes others expect instant replies or constant availability because your phone is always at hand. Clearly but kindly communicate your new approach. Try scripts such as:

- "I turn off notifications after 7pm to wind down—if it's urgent, please text."
- "I'm taking a social media break for my mental health."
- "I'll reply to work emails during business hours."

- "I'm less available on weekends but will check in on Monday."

You can also use status messages or email auto-replies: "Thanks for reaching out! I'm offline after 6pm and will get back to you tomorrow." These gentle cues set expectations and protect your peace.

Track and Notice the Effects

As you experiment with digital boundaries, observe the impact—not just on anxiety but on sleep, mood and focus. Consider keeping a brief seven-day "digital detox" log each evening, jotting down time spent on screens, boundaries you kept and how you felt physically or emotionally. Did you feel less on edge? Sleep better? Have more energy? One reader noticed that muting notifications for just a week left her calmer each day: "I didn't even realize how anxious I'd gotten until the pings stopped."

Try this prompt: Identify one thing you can enjoy or pay attention to without digital distraction—maybe the taste of a meal, a longer talk with your kids, or just your own thoughts while walking outside. Write it down or say it aloud as a reminder that these boundaries make space for real life.

Remember Your Right to Set Boundaries

You're allowed to protect your peace—both online and off. Your worth isn't tied to rapid replies or staying constantly informed.

As this chapter closes, remember: Digital boundaries aren't about missing out; they help you regain control of your attention, rest and calm. Step by step, you'll make room for what matters most—your well-being. Next, we'll explore how to recognize decision fatigue and rebuild confidence when anxiety influences your choices.

Chapter 12

High-Functioning Anxiety—When No One Knows You're Struggling

Managing the Mask—Tools for Private Strugglers

You know the scenario: You're the one who answers emails first, keeps track of forms, volunteers for extra work, juggles schedules and never misses a deadline. People praise your efficiency and composure—meanwhile, you're just barely staying afloat. This is high-functioning anxiety: You appear to thrive while internally battling constant worry and tension. The calm you project masks the chaos beneath.

The "mask" of high-functioning anxiety is incredibly convincing. You excel at seeming organized and reliable, even as your mind spirals into worst-case scenarios. Perhaps you obsessively prepare for meetings, triple-check details, or rewrite messages until they're perfect. Maybe you plan for every outcome, not only out of habit but out of fear of being caught unprepared. This drive comes from perfectionism, relentless people-pleasing and the inability to truly rest. The mask isn't about deceiving others; it's about survival. You want to feel steady, avoid letting others down and keep your own fears in check.

A reader once shared, "I'm the one who gets it all done, but inside I'm exhausted from treading water." This deep fatigue isn't just about work or obligations; it's the result of never letting your guard down. The traits of high-functioning anxiety—perfectionism, over-preparation, chronic people-pleasing and guilt over rest—often look like strengths on the outside. Even when you try to rest, your mind is busy with regrets or replaying conversations, and "good enough" never feels safe.

Wearing this mask has a genuine emotional cost. It can leave you with persistent imposter syndrome: The fear that if people discovered how much effort it takes just to appear "together," they'd see the reality of your struggle. You may fear being "found out" or believe your value depends on hiding your anxiety. The loneliness of being unseen is heavy; you might feel isolated in a room full of people or even with family, questioning whether your struggle is valid since you function so well.

Let me say this clearly: Your struggle is real, even if it's invisible to others. Your productivity doesn't negate your suffering and showing up doesn't mean you don't need breaks or support. High-functioning anxiety is hidden from most, but it matters—and deserves compassion.

So how can you cope when you can't remove the mask? Discreet, practical tools can help you stay grounded anytime, anywhere. One is micro-grounding: Silently press your thumb to each fingertip in turn, focusing on the physical sensation. This small act interrupts racing thoughts and anchors you in the present (see [source 1]). Alternatively, focus on your feet, feeling the ground beneath you—a subtle reminder that you are safe.

A quiet anchoring phrase, like "I can do this moment by moment," can help you stay present and prevent overwhelm. Repeat it silently whenever needed. If anxiety spikes during meetings or social events, pick a visual anchor (a clock, a spot on the wall) and rest your gaze there for a few seconds to reset. These strategies aren't about hiding your anxiety—they help you function when you can't step away.

You might wonder if— and when— it's right to take off the mask and share how you truly feel. That's a personal decision. Sometimes opening up feels daunting; sometimes it brings relief. If you choose to confide in someone, prepared scripts can help: "I'm having a hard time, but I have ways to cope," or "Sometimes I feel anxious, but I'm working on it." You don't have to share your whole story—choose one trusted friend, partner, therapist, or colleague who has demonstrated kindness and discretion.

Selective disclosure can be empowering. It gives you agency over your story in ways anxiety often takes away. Remember: Sharing your experience is a choice, not an obligation. Protecting your privacy is valid self-care.

Interactive Reflection: Is Your Mask on Too Tight?

Check in with yourself—no self-judgment.

- Do you often feel drained after socializing or working, even when it goes well?
- Do compliments about your organization or composure make you uneasy?
- Do you repeatedly analyze past conversations?
- Is it difficult to rest without feeling lazy?
- Are you afraid others would think less of you if they knew how anxious you feel?

If so, acknowledge that high-functioning anxiety often hides behind high achievement. You're not alone.

Allow yourself—at least once today—to drop the mask for just a minute. Step outside, close your eyes and breathe deeply, focusing on your body rather than your performance.

Your worth isn't tied to seeming unbothered or being hyper-productive. It's okay to be seen—or to choose privacy until you're ready. You have permission to rest beneath the mask, even if only briefly and only for yourself.

The "Invisible Load" Check-In

Everyday life comes with a weight you can't always see—the invisible load you carry from the moment your eyes open. This isn't just about tasks on a to-do list or what's written on your calendar. The invisible load is the tangled web of mental reminders, emotional care and social responsibility that you manage silently. It's the endless cycle of thinking ahead, keeping tabs on everyone's needs and adjusting your own actions so nothing falls through the cracks. You're not just remembering your child's dentist appointment; you're juggling birthdays for the whole extended family, prepping for meetings, anticipating what your boss or partner might want and making sure the fridge is stocked. The world often praises you for being the one who "keeps it all running." Yet no one stops to ask how heavy it all feels.

A friend of mine once described it perfectly: "I keep all the plates spinning—at work, at home, with friends—but no one realizes how heavy it feels." That hit home for me. Maybe you're nodding along because you recognize yourself in those words. The invisible load shows up in small moments—like remembering to text a friend good luck before her interview, planning every family vacation detail, or double-checking that everyone else's needs are met before you finally sit down. It also sneaks into how you self-monitor: Adjusting your tone in meetings to seem approachable, dressing a certain way for school pickup, or mentally rehearsing every conversation just to keep things smooth.

It's easy to underestimate just how much energy all this takes. Over time, this hidden burden builds up and can leave you feeling drained, scattered, or even resentful. The tricky part is that most people don't see any of it. They see you as organized, dependable, maybe even unflappable. They don't see the constant mental checklist running in your mind or the way you quietly anticipate everyone's needs—often at the expense of your own peace.

To help lighten this load, I recommend a structured "invisible load" check-in. Find a quiet moment—maybe in the car before heading inside, or while waiting for water to boil. Start by listing everything you're holding in your mind right now. Don't filter or edit—write down every responsibility, worry, reminder and expectation that comes to mind, no matter how small. Include things like "remember to buy birthday candles," "prep snacks for soccer," "schedule yearly checkup," or even "act upbeat for coworkers." If it's in your head or heart, it belongs on the list.

Once everything is out in the open, take a look at each item. Which ones leave you feeling most tense or anxious? Circle or underline those that spark the strongest physical or emotional response. Maybe planning meals fills you with dread or tracking everyone's schedules feels endless. Next, rate each item on a scale from 1 to 5—1 being light or routine, 5 being completely overwhelming or draining. This isn't about judging yourself for what feels hard; it's about clarity and honesty.

Now comes the part that most people skip: Actually doing something with what you've found. Look at the highest-rated tasks—what can be delegated, postponed, or let go? It's okay to say no to one new task this week. If a committee at work asks for volunteers and your plate is already full, try responding with, "I'd love to help another time, but I can't take anything else on right now." If managing a family task is too much, say, "Can someone else handle dinner on Thursday?" Even letting go of something tiny—like not sending out reminders to a group chat—counts as lightening your load.

Self-compassion is vital here. It's natural to feel guilty about passing things off or prioritizing your own mental space. Try gentle scripts with yourself: "It's okay for me to need help," or "Some things can wait." Choose just one action this week—delegate a task, drop a non-urgent responsibility, or simply acknowledge that not everything needs to be perfect. Each small step matters.

To make this check-in routine and not just a one-time event, set a weekly or monthly reminder in your calendar: "Invisible Load Review." Use it as a gentle checkpoint, not another chore. Ask yourself: What am I carrying right now? What can be put down for a while? Over time, checking in like this helps prevent overload before it takes hold. It also builds the habit of noticing and naming your efforts—not just what's visible to others.

I once heard from a reader who began doing these check-ins every Sunday evening. She told me, "My check-ins helped me realize I was doing enough—and I started giving myself permission to rest." That's powerful. Sometimes what you need most isn't advice or another strategy—it's simply permission to stop carrying so much alone.

If you take away anything from this section, let it be this: Not everything has to be carried at once. You're allowed to put things down. You matter as much as the people you care for and the roles you fill. Your invisible labour is real—even if the world doesn't acknowledge it out loud.

As we move forward into the next chapter, remember that honouring your limits isn't weakness—it's wisdom. Lightening your invisible load makes space for real rest and genuine connection, both with yourself and those around you.

Chapter 13

Decision Fatigue—Making Choices When You're Overwhelmed

The 3-Step "Good Enough" Decision Formula

Imagine standing tired and hungry in the grocery store aisle, paralyzed by dinner options like chicken, salmon, or pasta. Minutes pass as you scroll recipes, indecisive and overwhelmed, ultimately regretting how long it took and doubting your choice. If this resonates, know that decision fatigue is real and it's even tougher for anxious minds.

Decision fatigue doesn't mean you're "bad at adulting" or innately indecisive—it's a normal brain response to too many choices, worsened by anxiety's need for certainty. When faced with nonstop decisions—from outfits to emails to text messages—your brain tires, making even basic choices feel overwhelming. Anxiety heightens this because it's wired for danger detection and regret avoidance. If you endlessly make pros and cons lists, poll friends, or avoid choices altogether, you're not alone.

Signs of decision fatigue include constant second-guessing, feeling paralyzed by options, procrastinating, or obsessing over previous decisions. Sometimes you freeze and avoid deciding; other times, you agree to things just to end the discomfort—only to instantly doubt yourself and revisit what you didn't choose. It's exhausting.

Quick Research Box: Why the Anxious Mind Craves Certainty

The anxious brain's main job is to keep you safe—alert for mistakes or danger. Each decision feels fraught because anxiety exaggerates the downside of picking "wrong." Research shows anxiety increases our craving for certainty and control, making routine choices feel high-stakes (see source 2 in APA list). This isn't laziness—it's just the brain's way of fending off regret or embarrassment. Unfortunately, real certainty is rare; "good enough" is usually enough.

So, how can you make decisions without spiralling? Try the "Good Enough" Decision Formula—a 3-step method designed for anxious brains. Forget chasing a perfect solution; "good enough" is often all you need.

Step one: Narrow your choices to just two or three real options. More choices mean more overwhelm. If choosing dinner, select two recipes and ignore the rest. If it's jobs or apartments, focus on your top contenders and let go of the idea there's a perfect, magical answer out there. Just narrowing options can greatly relieve your mind and prevent endless scrolling.

Step two: Set a timer for the decision. For small things—like lunch or which shirt to buy—give yourself one to five minutes. For bigger decisions—like jobs or trips—set a 24-hour deadline. Timers prevent rumination and force forward motion. Tell yourself, "I have five minutes to pick; then I move on." If you stall, shorten the time.

Step three: Make your choice, act and commit—not reopening the decision for a set period. After you choose, give yourself permission to let it be done for now. Tell your brain it's okay to move on—no replaying the issue while brushing your teeth. You can always adjust later, but for now, trust yourself to stick with the decision.

Throughout, practice self-compassion. Before deciding, remind yourself: "Any choice is a step forward—I can course correct if needed." During the process, keep it gentle: "Perfection isn't necessary. I'm doing my best." Afterward, pair your choice with a physical cue like a deep breath, a stretch, or placing your hand on your heart as a grounding ritual to reinforce to your body that it's safe to move on. As one reader shared, "Choosing good enough meals cut my stress in half." Most choices aren't as high-stakes as anxiety makes them seem.

Troubleshooting is key—especially as anxiety pulls you back into indecision. If you feel compelled to revisit the decision or poll others again, pause and acknowledge it mindfully: "I want to reopen this because I'm uncomfortable with uncertainty." Name the feeling, then gently redirect your focus—even for a few minutes.

Sometimes, it helps to have a "decision buddy." This isn't someone who helps you decide (that can become another way to dodge your own judgment), but someone you check in with afterward. They can celebrate your follow-through or remind you why you made your choice. This accountability can make things less lonely and easier to keep moving forward.

Reward yourself for completing the process, no matter how minor the decision. After deciding, treat yourself—have tea, watch your favourite show, or take a quiet break outside. This soothes your nervous system and helps retrain your brain to value the act of deciding, not perfection.

Interactive Reflection: Your Decision Fatigue Checklist

Set aside two minutes to jot down three draining decisions—big or small. For each, note if you've (a) polled others, (b) second-guessed endlessly, or (c) avoided action. Pick one and apply the Good Enough

Decision Formula this week: narrow your options, set a timer, act and commit, then reward yourself for moving ahead.

Experiencing decision fatigue doesn't mean anything is wrong with you—your brain is just working overtime to protect you from regret. With practice and self-compassion, "good enough" choices become freeing and achievable.

"What Matters Now?"—A Quick Clarity Exercise

Anxiety can make your daily life feel like a noisy, never-ending game show, with every buzzer going off at once. Each task shouts for attention. Laundry, work emails, family texts, dinner plans, a forgotten bill—everything blurs together and feels equally urgent. In these moments, it's easy to lose perspective and believe every single thing on your list deserves panic-level focus. But the truth is, not everything matters right now. Most of us have lived through afternoons or entire days where the weight of "all the things" made it impossible to start anything. I remember one client who told me, "I felt like I had 20 things to do, but when I stopped and really asked what mattered now, only one was actually urgent." Her shoulders dropped just realizing that.

Anxiety tricks you into thinking every decision and every to-do is a five-alarm fire. It's a survival instinct gone haywire. Your mind craves order and certainty, so when you're faced with a mountain of choices, it sounds the alarm for each one—just in case. This is why you might find yourself staring at your phone, paralyzed by competing pings and reminders, or bouncing from one half-finished task to another. It's not laziness or lack of willpower; it's your brain trying to keep you safe by treating all uncertainty as a risk. When everything feels like a crisis, nothing gets done.

In my own life, I've learned that asking "What matters most right now?" can be the rope that pulls me out of the quicksand. This question isn't about productivity hacks or squeezing more into an already packed day. It's about finding clarity in the chaos and letting yourself off the hook for not doing it all at once. Focus is a form of self-care—it's an act of kindness to your nervous system and a gift to your future self.

Here's an exercise for those moments when your brain won't stop spinning and you can't tell what truly needs attention. First, pause and take three slow breaths. Really breathe—not the shallow kind that anxiety loves, but deep inhales and longer exhales that signal safety to your body. Even if you have to hide in the bathroom or step into a hallway, give yourself this small break. Next, grab whatever is handy—paper, sticky note, or your phone—and list out every choice or task swirling in your head. Don't censor or judge; just dump it out quickly. Let the messy list be as long or short as it needs.

Now comes the sorting. Look over your list and circle the one or two items that will make the biggest positive impact or bring immediate relief if handled first. Maybe it's paying a bill before a deadline, sending one email that stops a problem from growing, or simply getting a snack if hunger is making things worse. Everything else? Mentally or physically set those aside for later. You have permission to let them wait—guilt-free. They're not vanishing forever; they're just not today's emergencies.

Anxiety will try to convince you that setting things aside is irresponsible. That's just old fear talking. You're not giving up—you're triaging like a skilled ER nurse. Most tasks can wait without disaster striking, even if anxiety says otherwise. One reader shared with me, "When I actually wrote it down, I realized most of my to-do list could wait." She was shocked to see how few items truly demanded her attention in that moment.

You don't have to rely on memory or willpower to stay anchored in this practice. Set a phone alarm labelled "What matters now?" for times when you're most likely to get overwhelmed—maybe late morning after meetings start piling up, or mid-afternoon when energy fades and demands multiply. Seeing that question pop up on your lock screen can be a gentle nudge back to reality when anxiety tries to drag you under again.

Repeat this exercise whenever life feels like too much—midday at work when everything is on fire, after school pick-up chaos, or at bedtime when the day's tasks chase you into the dark. Over time, it rewires your brain to recognize which problems are real fires and which are just smoke.

A priority mantra can help even more when overwhelm peaks. Short phrases like "First things first," "One thing at a time," or "Progress, not perfection" are easy to remember and repeat under stress. Write yours on sticky notes around your space—on your laptop, bathroom mirror, or next to your bed—or set it as your phone background for an extra reminder during tense moments. These mantras serve as anchors, pulling you back from the urge to spiral.

At the end of each day—no matter how messy or scattered it felt—pause and ask: What truly mattered today? What can I let go for tomorrow? This reflection helps you see that not every unchecked box spells disaster and that your value isn't tied to getting everything done all at once.

All these steps are about giving yourself permission to focus on what's truly important while letting the rest fall away for now. You're not slacking—you're prioritizing with intention. The more you practice this exercise, the more natural it becomes to filter out noise and move forward with confidence.

As we close this chapter on decision overwhelm and finding clarity amid chaos, remember: It's not about being perfect or keeping every plate spinning without pause. It's about learning which plates matter most in each moment—and knowing it's okay to set a few down until you're ready. Next up: Building habits that support lasting change, even when anxiety tries to pull you back into old patterns.

Chapter 14

Navigating Setbacks—Staying Resilient When Anxiety Returns

The Reset Ritual—Bouncing Back from Bad Days

We all have rough days—waking up groggy, spilling coffee, facing unexpected frustrations like rude comments, tantrums, or surprise bills. When this happens, it can feel like all your progress with anxiety management vanishes: Tension rises, emotions spill over and you wonder if you're back at square one. It's common to mistake a bad day for a total loss, but the reality is, setbacks are normal—it's just how anxiety ebbs and flows. Everyone faces them, regardless of progress made.

Anxiety is cyclical. Even after weeks or months of steady improvement, setbacks happen to everyone. As one reader put it, "Even after weeks of progress, I had a meltdown—but it didn't erase my growth." A tough moment or bad day doesn't undo your hard work—it simply means your mind and body need something different right now. Perfection isn't required; recovering after setbacks with self-compassion is what matters.

So what usually triggers these tough days? It's rarely anything dramatic—often it's just basic life: Poor sleep, unexpected stressors, feeling sick, or hormonal shifts throwing off your mood. Sometimes it's a combination—one rough night leads to an even rougher day at work or home. These aren't personal flaws—they're simply part of being human. Remind yourself: "A tough day is a pause, not a failure."

So, how do you recover when anxiety flares up? That's where a "reset ritual" can help. The goal isn't to fix everything instantly, but to give yourself permission to pause, regroup and gently move forward.

Step one: Pause. Literally stop for a moment—thirty seconds is enough—and acknowledge what you're feeling. Say it out loud if you can: "Today was hard. I'm struggling." This brings awareness and invites self-compassion.

Step two: Offer yourself comfort. Don't overthink it; just choose something soothing. Maybe that's holding a warm mug, wrapping up in a soft blanket, playing calming music, or simply being quiet for a bit. The goal isn't to distract from discomfort but to let your nervous system know it's safe. If comfort feels distant, try something simple—wash your face, change into cozy clothes, or light a candle.

Step three: ask yourself what you really need right now—rest, connection, or movement? Sometimes you might need to rest, skipping chores or plans. Other times you might want support, like sending a quick text to someone who understands or letting your partner know you're struggling. Movement can also help: Take a slow walk, stretch, or step outside for some fresh air.

Step four: Choose one gentle next step. Not a list—just one simple action that moves you forward again. That could mean taking a shower, having a snack, texting a friend, tidying a small corner, or taking a few breaths outdoors. The simplicity is what helps—don't try to reclaim the whole day, just nudge yourself gently onward.

To make hard days easier, prepare a reset kit for yourself. This doesn't need to be fancy—just keep a few comforting things in one place. Your kit could include a favourite snack, a kind note to yourself, a soothing scent, cozy socks, or a playlist that soothes you. Put your kit somewhere easy to reach: Bedside table, work drawer, or your car.

Reset Reflection: Gentle Journaling for Setbacks

Setbacks are lighter when approached with kindness, not blame. Use your journal, phone, or even a scrap of paper to try this prompt: "What can I learn from today, without judgment?" Track any patterns—did poor sleep or skipping breakfast make things tougher? Did stress pile on unexpectedly? Use this space to be curious, not critical. If you see sleep was an issue, plan an earlier bedtime—not as punishment, but as self-care.

Build a "bounce-back" list: Write down three things that helped today (even little ones, like going outside or texting a friend) and three things to try next time things get rough. This isn't about strict rules but about developing self-understanding and practical options for the future.

Setbacks are simply part of life—they don't erase your progress or say anything about your worth. Every time you pause, offer yourself compassion, honestly reflect and take one small step—no matter how tiny—you strengthen your resilience.

Progress Over Perfection—Tracking Tiny Wins

Perfectionism loves to creep into anxiety recovery, whispering that if you aren't making big, sweeping changes every day, you're not moving forward. It's a voice that insists only flawless days or dramatic improvements count as "real" progress. Maybe you know that voice well—the one that tells you if you take a step back, you've lost it all. I've had to work hard to quiet that critic and I know you have too.

The truth is, progress is not a straight line and it definitely isn't about perfection. It's about a whole bunch of awkward, beautiful, tiny steps—many of them so small they barely get noticed unless we shine a light on them.

I remember talking with someone who once said, "I used to think only big wins counted, but now I track every small victory." That stuck with me. Because it's those little efforts—getting out of bed when anxiety wanted you to hide, sending yourself a kind text when your mind went dark, taking one steady breath in a tense meeting—that really add up. When perfectionism takes the wheel, you miss these moments completely. You forget that choosing to speak gently to yourself instead of spiralling in criticism is a win. That getting through a rough morning, even if you felt far from calm, is worthy of celebration. Perfectionism tricks you into thinking nothing counts unless it's picture-perfect, but that's not how healing works.

So, what if you started giving yourself credit for every step forward—even the ones that look tiny or uneven? This is where a "tiny wins tracker" becomes your secret weapon. It doesn't have to be fancy. Grab a notepad, open a notes app on your phone, or keep a jar on your counter with marbles or stones. The medium doesn't matter; what matters is the act of noticing and honouring your own effort. Each day, jot down one thing you did for your well-being. Just one. Didn't have a panic attack at work even though your hands were shaking? That counts. Paused before snapping at your kids? That counts, too. Sent an honest text to a friend about needing space? Absolutely counts.

Your tracker might fill up with entries like: "Got dressed even when I wanted to stay in pajamas," "Took my meds," "Chose silence instead of doomscrolling," or "Texted my check-in buddy." Some days will have bigger moments—maybe you finally made that doctor's appointment or tried a new grounding exercise—but most days will be made up of these small, gritty wins. If you're more visual, grab some stickers and put one on your calendar for every win, or drop a marble in a jar each time you do something kind for yourself. Some people like digital trackers—there are plenty of apps for mood and habit tracking if that's your thing. The point isn't the method; it's the acknowledgment.

Celebration doesn't have to mean throwing a party every time you pause to breathe. It can be simple—a quick happy dance in your kitchen after logging a win, playing a favourite "victory" song in the car on your way home, or just taking a second to say out loud, "That mattered." If you have someone safe—a friend, partner, or therapist—share your wins with them now and then. Let their encouragement add fuel to your progress. Sometimes I'll just do a little fist pump after marking something down—a private moment of pride that no one else sees but me.

As the days go by and the tracker grows longer, it becomes proof of your resilience—a living record of all the ways you keep showing up for yourself when anxiety tries to knock you down. On those days when you feel like nothing is working and you're moving backward, pull out your tracker and look at what's there. You might be surprised at how many wins have piled up, even on weeks that felt impossible. Circle the ones from tough days and let them remind you that setbacks don't erase progress—they reveal just how persistent and strong you actually are.

Reviewing your tracker shouldn't be another box to check or chore to dread. Make it something gentle and kind—a weekly Sunday evening ritual or a monthly coffee break where you look back and notice growth. Maybe set an alert on your phone as a reminder to pause and reflect. Notice patterns: Are there certain types of wins that show up again and again? Are there stretches where things felt harder but you still kept going? Use this review not as a way to judge yourself but as evidence that healing is happening—even if it doesn't look like the way perfectionism says it should.

A tiny wins tracker is more than just a tool; it's an act of rebellion against the lie that only perfection is progress. It's how you teach yourself, over time, that every bit of effort matters and deserves respect. Recovery from anxiety isn't about never stumbling—it's about learning how to take credit for standing up again, no matter how many times anxiety tries to pull you off course.

So here's what matters most: Every step counts. Every effort matters. Whether today's win was huge or almost invisible, it belongs on your tracker. When setbacks happen—and they will—these tiny wins become your proof that resilience lives in all the small moments when you choose to keep going.

As we wrap up this chapter, remember: Progress is about keeping track of the steps you take, not about walking in a straight line. In the next chapter, we'll talk about building habits that actually last—so all these small wins can become part of everyday life, not just something you reach for during setbacks.

Chapter 15

The Power of Micro-Habits— Building Lasting Change

5-Minute Morning Rituals for Calm

Imagine your alarm goes off and before your feet touch the floor, your brain jumps into a relentless mental checklist—emails, chores, family obligations—with anxiety hitting before you even start your day. Those first five minutes set your tone, nudging you toward either stability or stress. Instead of letting mornings spiral into autopilot overwhelm, try reclaiming just five minutes—before demands set in—to lay a foundation for calm. This doesn't require perfection or an elaborate "miracle morning." A simple ritual sending your brain a signal—"You're safe; you've got this"—can have lasting effects.

Why does a quick morning ritual matter? Science shows your brain is highly sensitive right after waking due to a hormonal surge—cortisol, dopamine, serotonin—all shaping mood and focus. Morning light stops melatonin and sharpens thinking. Gentle movement or breathing boosts mood-regulating chemicals. Repeating a simple, calming action each day forms a pattern that soothes your nervous system, teaching your brain the day is manageable and lowering that instant anxiety that feels like you're behind before starting ([64]).

For many anxious adults, mornings begin loaded with dread. One reader once admitted checking her phone first thing always made her chest tight, but switching to three slow breaths and a little sunlight made her steadier all day—even tough moments didn't hit as hard. The goal isn't an Instagram-ready routine but rather a flexible menu of micro-habits that fit your reality—even if you have only two minutes.

Let's rethink "morning ritual." You don't need a 30-minute meditation, a gratitude journal, or sunrise yoga (unless that's genuinely for you). This is about a toolkit—a few short, customizable habits for real mornings, not an ideal schedule. Each is under five minutes, requires nothing fancy and you can swap, combine, or just choose one, depending on what your morning brings.

"Sunlight Start" is a favourite: Before checking your phone, open a window or step outside for a minute. Natural light tells your internal clock it's time to wake and helps shift your brain from night to day. If the weather's bad, stand by a window and get whatever daylight's available.

"Body Wake-Up" isn't a workout; while waiting for coffee or the shower, stretch arms overhead, then lean side to side. Pair with three slow breaths: inhale, stretch, exhale. This movement oxygenates your body and releases overnight tension.

Music can be another strong anchor. Pick a "Calm Cue"—a gentle alarm or soothing song—as you get ready or prep breakfast. This signals the brain to start the day gently, not jarringly. Try using your favourite calm song as your alarm for an immediate mood boost.

Take coffee or tea—the sacred "Mindful Sip." Instead of gulping it down while multitasking, pause and experience the first sips: Feel the warmth, savour the taste and let the act of drinking slow you down, rather than diving into the next task.

How do you make these habits stick in busy mornings? Habit stacking is a proven strategy ([36]). Anchor a new ritual to something you do every day. For example, after brushing your teeth, pause for three deep breaths before leaving the bathroom. Stick a reminder note on your mirror ("I am safe to move slowly") or set your water bottle out so you drink first thing. When tied to existing habits, these micro-rituals become almost automatic. Maybe play your Calm Cue song while making lunches or stretch before your shower—it's not more on your to-do list, just woven into what you already do.

Don't underestimate the power of a small celebration in building consistency. Track your streaks however you want—calendar checkmarks, app taps, or even stickers ([68]). If you miss a day, don't quit; just start again the next morning. As one reader shared, "I missed my morning ritual last Tuesday and felt off—but on Wednesday, I simply picked it up again." It's not about perfect streaks, but about returning to the habit and noticing gradual progress.

Notice how these micro-rituals influence your mood or anxiety as the days pass. Are your mornings less rushed? Does sunlight or music make meetings or school drop-offs less stressful? Reflect, because even small tweaks can bring surprising relief.

Morning Ritual Menu—Interactive Reflection

Take five minutes tonight to list which micro-habits appeal to you (or create your own):

- Sunlight Start
- Body Wake-Up
- Calm Cue
- Mindful Sip

Pick one for tomorrow. Attach it to an existing morning habit (brushing teeth, making coffee) and at week's end, circle a word that describes how your mornings felt: Frantic, steady, hopeful, scattered —anything honest. Some days may unravel, but each attempt plants a seed for calmer mornings ahead.

Evening Check-Out – Closing the Day with Self-Compassion

Winding down at night is where anxiety loves to sneak in. When everything gets quiet, your mind runs highlight reels of what went wrong, things left undone, or conversations that didn't land quite right. If you find yourself lying in bed replaying every awkward moment or mistake, you aren't alone. That restless, unsettled feeling is your nervous system's way of holding on to the day's stresses. What if you gave yourself permission to close the mental tabs, just like you'd power down an overworked computer? An intentional evening check-out isn't about perfection or squeezing more productivity from a tired brain. It's a gentle signal: "You made it through. Now it's safe to rest."

When you build a small, intentional wind-down into your nights, you help your mind—and body—shift from alert mode to a state where actual rest is possible. The brain needs a clear signal that the day is over before it lets go of vigilance. A reader once messaged me, "I realized I kept replaying emails and to-do lists at midnight. My evening check-out gave me permission to stop replaying the day's mistakes." There's something powerful about acknowledging the day, even if it was messy and then drawing a line under it.

You don't need an hour or a complicated bedtime routine. Just a few minutes and some honesty. Try these simple rituals:

Start with a "Gratitude Glance." Name one thing you handled well— even if it's as basic as "I answered that tough text" or "I got out of bed when I wanted to hide." This isn't toxic positivity. It's about noticing survival and effort, not glossing over pain. If nothing comes to mind, that's okay—sometimes just showing up counts.

Next, consider a "Let Go List." Write down one worry or regret from the day—a quick scribble on a notepad by your bed or even a voice memo on your phone. Saying, "I wish I hadn't snapped at my partner," or "I'm still worried about that bill" helps move it from swirling thoughts into something you can see or hear. You don't have to solve it now. You're just parking it outside your head until morning.

There's also the "Gentle Touch" ritual. Place your hand over your heart or gently on your cheek. Pair this with a soft phrase: "Today is done. I did enough," or whatever feels right to you. This physical touch, paired with kind words, sends signals of safety to your brain, helping unwind tension stored in the body.

Screens are often the last thing we look at before sleep, but they keep our nervous systems wired. Try a "Screen-Free Minute" before bed. Set your phone aside for sixty seconds and focus on slow breathing or on something calming—a soft pillow, your pet's steady breath, the weight of a blanket. This break cues your mind that it's time for you to power down.

Make this process personal by creating your own bedtime script or mantra. Use a simple template: "Tonight I choose to rest. Whatever is unfinished can wait until tomorrow." One reader taped her mantra above her nightstand: "I close my eyes on today; tomorrow will take care of itself." If you prefer, record yourself saying your check-out phrase and play it back as you settle into bed. Hearing your own voice offering kindness can be surprisingly soothing.

Consistency is more important than perfection here and tracking these rituals can help them stick. Pair your check-out with something relaxing—herbal tea, soft lighting, or your favourite scent (lavender spray or clean sheets work wonders). After each check-out, mark a star or sticker on your calendar. There's no need for streaks—if you miss a night or just repeat your mantra in bed without all the steps, it still counts. One reader told me, "On rough days, I just whisper my mantra under the covers and call it good."

Over time, these acts grow into cues for safety and closure. You'll start noticing patterns: Maybe sleep comes easier, or anxiety doesn't spiral as much at night. Some nights will still be restless—that doesn't mean you've failed. The goal is not perfect calm but building a habit of self-kindness that slowly changes how you feel about ending the day.

If you want to reflect more deeply, keep a simple log for a week: Did you do your evening check-out? How did you sleep? Was anxiety louder or quieter? You might notice that even on tough days, this ritual makes things just a little lighter.

The real reward isn't a perfect night's sleep or waking up refreshed every morning (though those are lovely side effects). It's learning to meet yourself at day's end without judgment—just recognition that you've done what you could with what you had.

Closing your day with self-compassion isn't an indulgence; it's maintenance for a mind that works overtime. Instead of expecting yourself to bounce back without ever powering down, this is how you teach your system to feel safe enough for real rest.

So as this chapter winds down, remember: Building lasting change comes from tiny, repeated acts—not grand gestures or perfect routines. Micro-habits like these work quietly in the background, making calm more possible tomorrow than it felt today. In the next chapter, we'll talk about building support and connection—because while self-kindness matters, nobody should have to carry this work alone.

Chapter 16

Seeking Help—When and How to Reach Out

Is It Time for Therapy?—Red Flags and Green Lights

You might find yourself sitting in your car, unable to go inside, mind circling the same worries again and again. Maybe you've tried podcasts, meditation, or every grounding exercise you know. You can appear "fine" to others, but deep down, nothing is changing. The days blur together and you start to wonder if this is just "normal" adulthood—or if it's time for something different.

It can be tough to distinguish between everyday anxiety and the point where professional support could really help. Yes, everyone feels stressed sometimes—deadlines, relationship bumps, parenting chaos. But sometimes anxiety takes root and begins to disrupt your life. Here's how to spot that line—without clinical jargon or intimidating labels.

Let's talk "red flags." These mean anxiety is now a long-term resident, not an occasional visitor. If your anxiety is persistent—lasts weeks or months—not just days, pay attention. Maybe you start avoiding things you used to handle, like calling out sick because work seems impossible, skipping social events, letting mail pile up. Panic attacks, especially if they alter your plans or strike in public, are another clue. Anxiety can erode basic self-care too: Skipping showers, poor eating habits, struggling to get out of bed. The most serious red flag is hopelessness—wishing you didn't have to wake up or thinking about self-harm, even fleetingly. These are urgent and deserve immediate support.

But there are also "green lights" for seeking help. Things don't have to be falling apart—maybe you're curious about therapy, or you've plateaued with self-help. Sometimes you simply want someone on your side for perspective and accountability. Even just wanting more for yourself is enough reason to seek support.

A story from a reader, Morgan, demonstrates this: "I used to say I was just tired or burned out. Then I realized I hadn't laughed or enjoyed anything in weeks. I knew that wasn't just stress and nothing I tried helped." That absence of relief or joy is a powerful signal.

Self-Reflection Checklist: "Am I…?"

Take a quiet moment and check in honestly. Use a 1–5 scale (1 = never/rarely; 5 = almost always), or jot notes for a week to see patterns. Are you…

- Avoiding people or activities you once enjoyed because of anxiety?
- Feeling anxious most days, for weeks at a time?
- Struggling with basic self-care (eating, sleeping, showering)?
- Feeling dread about everyday tasks (emails, bills, errands)?
- Experiencing physical symptoms (racing heart, stomach issues) that persist despite usual coping?
- Having trouble focusing or feeling "foggy" almost daily?
- Getting panic attacks or frequent spikes of fear?

- Losing hope or interest in things that mattered before?
- Feeling life is pointless or hard to keep up with?
- Wishing someone else could take over so you could rest?

If several answers land high—or any safety or hopelessness questions feel true—it's time to consider reaching out.

It's normal to feel awkward—or even scared—about therapy. Many believe therapy is "only for people really struggling," or that seeing a therapist means you've failed at handling life alone. You might wonder: Is my anxiety "bad enough" for therapy? The answer is simple: Therapy isn't about being "bad enough" or hitting bottom. It's about wanting support and trying something new when old strategies don't work.

Another common worry: What if the therapist thinks I'm overreacting? Maybe you've been shrugged off before: "You're just sensitive" or "Everyone feels like this sometimes." But a good therapist listens without judgment and meets you right where you are.

And the big one: Does going to therapy mean I've failed? This myth tells us we should fix everything alone and that asking for help is weak. The truth is the opposite—seeking help is courageous. It shows you care enough about yourself (and your family) to try something new.

If making an appointment feels overwhelming, try a micro-action. Browse a few local therapy websites—not to book, just to see options. Write down your biggest worry about therapy and tuck it away for later. If talking is too hard, send a private email or text a trusted friend who has tried therapy—ask what surprised them most. Many communities offer free groups or online info sessions; attending one, even just to listen, can ease fears.

Any step that feels manageable is enough. Even saving a hotline number or bookmarking a support website counts—just in case one day reaching out feels possible.

Self-Assessment Interactive Prompt: Your Readiness Reflection

Pick one question from the checklist that resonates. Write what makes it hard or scary to discuss with someone else. Then write one thing that would make seeking help easier—maybe knowing others feel this way, having a gentle script, or believing your story deserves space.

You can revisit these reflections as often as needed. When you're ready—even if you aren't sure what to say—remember: Reaching out doesn't have to be perfect; it just has to be honest enough for today.

How to Find (and Talk to) a Therapist Who Gets It

Finding a therapist can feel as overwhelming as choosing from endless cereal boxes—so many options with different promises. The best approach is to break the process into small, manageable steps that help you avoid feeling stuck. Start by considering what type of support best fits your current life. Some people prefer in-person sessions for the structure or reality of face-to-face interaction. Others need the flexibility of online therapy to fit busy schedules or avoid travel fatigue. You might be interested in group therapy for peer support, or you may want a specialist experienced in trauma, parenting, or social anxiety. There's no right or wrong choice—just what matches your needs.

Then, start gathering therapist options. Use online directories like Psychology Today, check your insurance provider's network, or ask trusted friends or family for recommendations. Community centres and religious groups may also keep lists. If reading endless profiles is tiring, try to select just three to consider further. Remember, you're not committing—just compiling possibilities.

Make a private "therapist wish list" of preferences. What qualities matter to you? Perhaps you want someone warm or nonjudgmental, experience with specific concerns (like anxiety or trauma), or cultural competence—someone who understands your background without much explaining. You may want a therapist who shares your gender, identity, faith, or life experience. Consider whether you prefer a more passive listener or someone who offers concrete strategies. Writing down some hopes can help clarify what support feels safest to you—even if you're not sure yet.

When ready to reach out, write a short script or email to make contact easier. No need to share your full story right away. Example: "Hi, I'm interested in therapy for anxiety and wanted to see if you have openings for new clients." If calling feels stressful, use email or an online contact form—many therapists expect and prefer this.

If you get voicemail, don't worry about leaving the perfect message. You might say: "Hello, my name is [first name]. I'm looking for support with anxiety and wondered if you're taking new clients. Please let me know how to move forward." If returned calls come at inconvenient moments, it's okay to let it go to voicemail and return the call when you feel ready.

Your first conversation—by phone, video, or in person—is your chance to ask questions that help you feel comfortable. You might ask:

- What is your experience working with anxiety?
- What is your general approach to therapy?
- How are sessions structured?
- Do you assign homework, or is the style more conversational?
- What should I expect in our first session?
- How do you maintain privacy and confidentiality?
- Have you worked with people from [your background/identity]?
- Are there specialties (like trauma, parenting, OCD)?
- How do you help clients who find it hard to open up?

Pay attention to how you feel during and after the conversation. Do you sense warmth and respect? Do they listen well? Are they clear and unhurried? Good signs are feeling heard and respected—never pressured or rushed. If you feel dismissed or judged, or if the pace feels too fast, that's a red flag. Trust your instincts—if something feels off, keep looking; a good fit is essential.

It's perfectly normal to "shop around." Therapists expect this and you deserve support that fits—not just whomever is available.

Obstacles like insurance confusion, high costs, long waits, or disappointing first meetings are common but not signals to give up. Many therapists offer sliding scale fees based on income, so ask: "Do you offer reduced rates?" If your insurance isn't accepted or wait times are long, consider teletherapy—which can be more affordable—local nonprofits, employee assistance programs, or community mental health organizations.

For money questions, try: "Can you walk me through your rates and payment options? Is there a sliding scale?" If a therapist isn't available soon, ask about cancellation lists or other recommendations.

If your first session isn't a match, remember it's normal—not a failure. Sometimes it takes meeting a few therapists to find the right one.

While finding support isn't always quick or easy, each attempt brings you closer to what you need. Every step—even reading this—is progress.

In summary: Decide which kind of support fits your life, collect a few therapist options, clarify your priorities, reach out with simple scripts and trust your gut throughout. If you encounter setbacks—like insurance issues, costs, or long waits—it's okay to pause, adjust and try again. You deserve care that matches your needs and makes anxiety less isolating. Up next, we'll discuss building a wider support network —because therapy helps, but community matters too.

Chapter 17

Your Support Network—Enlisting Allies (and Educating Them)

The Partner's Guide—Explaining Anxiety to Loved Ones

Imagine a typical weekend: The dishes pile up, texts go unanswered, the kids squabble nearby and your partner glances over, a bit perplexed or helpless. You want to explain what's going on inside, but the words just aren't there. Anxiety often feels like a private storm—others can't see it and your loved ones are left guessing, sometimes feeling hurt or unsure how to help. If discussing your anxiety with your partner feels awkward or overwhelming, you're not alone.

Opening up about anxiety isn't dumping all your worries at once, nor is it about confessing weakness. Instead, it means letting your loved one understand your inner world a bit better, so they don't have to guess or misread your moods. Pick a calm, quiet moment—after dinner, during a walk, or settling in for the night—to start the conversation. An easy opener: "There's something important I want to share about how anxiety shows up for me." This invites mutual problem solving, not blame or rescue.

Use "I" statements. Say, "I feel overwhelmed when plans change suddenly," instead of, "You always make me feel anxious when you..." This centers the experience on your own feelings, reducing defensiveness and showing you're responsible for your emotions, not blaming your partner.

Metaphors are helpful for bridging understanding. You might say, "Anxiety for me is like a fire alarm blaring, even when there's no fire—just burnt toast." This makes anxiety less mysterious and easier to relate to. Your partner may only see the surface—pacing, zoning out, irritability, or avoidance. Let them know these reactions are not directed at them, but are symptoms of your mind's overactive alarm.

Describe how anxiety appears for you physically, mentally and emotionally. Perhaps your chest tightens if plans change or your mind races with worst-case scenarios at family events. You may become quiet or irritable, not out of distance, but because your nervous system is in overdrive. The more specifically you paint this picture, the more your partner can recognize, "This is anxiety—not me, not our relationship."

Interactive Element: My "What Anxiety Feels Like for Me" Worksheet

Spend five minutes answering these prompts (or write your own) and share them with your partner in a calm moment:

1. When I'm anxious, I feel it in my body as: (e.g., racing heart, tense muscles)
2. My mind reacts by: (e.g., overthinking, zoning out)
3. Emotionally, I tend to: (e.g., withdraw, get irritable)
4. What I wish you knew: (e.g., I need space; I want comfort but can't ask)
5. Things that help: (e.g., quiet company, gentle touch, time alone)
6. Things that don't: (e.g., being told to relax, forced solutions)

After sharing, give your partner clear guidance on how to support you and set boundaries. Well-meaning loved ones may try to fix everything, but that often backfires. Be specific: Do validate with, "That sounds tough," or just sit with you. Do ask, "How can I help? Would you like company, a distraction, or space?" Don't say, "Just relax," or "You're overreacting." Don't rush into problem-solving or minimize your feelings. Your experience is real, even if it doesn't always make sense from the outside.

A practical step: Create a Support Menu—a brief list of strategies that help when anxiety spikes, such as:

- Give me a hug
- Sit quietly with me
- Offer a funny distraction
- Ask if I'd like space
- Make me some tea
- Remind me of something helpful from the past

You can share this list in advance or keep it handy on your phone.

Sometimes, even with the best intentions, things don't go smoothly. Partners may get frustrated or not understand right away, or they might forget what to do. Misunderstandings are normal—building understanding takes time, not one perfect conversation. If things go sideways, revisit the discussion later: "This is new for us both. Let's keep working on it." Sometimes, sharing an article, book, or story is more effective than any clinical explanation. Couples therapy can help if communication is difficult (Source 2, APA).

Personal stories can be powerful. One reader recounted that her husband finally understood her panic attacks only after she described freezing during a high school exam—he remembered his own nerves and connected the dots.

Remember, opening up is not about making your partner responsible for your anxiety—it's inviting them into your experience so they can support you in ways that are genuinely helpful, not accidentally hurtful (Source 1, APA). These talks require patience and repetition, but every moment of honesty helps build trust and partnership.

Building Your "Check-In Buddy" System

Anxiety often makes you feel isolated, even if your life seems full. It's easy to get trapped in overthinking, doubting your progress and feeling like no one understands. That's why having a "check-in buddy" can be so helpful. This person isn't a therapist and isn't there to fix everything—think of them as a peer who understands what it's like to struggle and who's willing to share honesty in both directions. They're here for real talk, not just the good moments.

Having a check-in buddy can transform the way you experience anxiety. Just sending or receiving a message like, "It's been a rough morning," or "I did my breathing exercise before work," can break through feelings of isolation. Instead of waiting for someone to notice you're struggling, you have built-in support. There's gentle accountability that encourages you to try new coping tools or stick with the ones that work. On tough days, knowing someone cares enough to check in can make all the difference. One reader shared, "My check-in buddy and I text three times a week about our wins and setbacks—it broke the cycle of hiding and made us both feel less alone."

Your choice of buddy matters more than you might expect. Look for someone trustworthy who won't share your private thoughts. They should be nonjudgmental and willing to listen without rushing to give advice, unless you ask. Reliability helps, too—you want someone who won't disappear for weeks at a time and who respects your boundaries about what you do or don't want to discuss. This person might be a close friend, a sibling, a coworker, or even someone from a support group.

Starting this kind of partnership may feel awkward if you're used to handling things alone. A simple approach is best: "I'm working on my anxiety and think having someone to check in with could help. Would you be open to being that person for me?" Or you could ask, "Could we exchange occasional updates on how we're doing? Just low-pressure check-ins?" Set expectations early with a trial period or low-stakes check-ins at first, so you both have space to find what feels helpful.

When it's time to check in, keep it simple and sustainable. Daily or weekly texts work for most people. A quick "How are you feeling on a scale of 1–10 today?" can open up honest conversation without much effort. Some people like a "win of the week" call or video chat to share something that went well and something that was hard. Others send prompts like reminders to use coping tools, self-care tips, or something funny to boost moods. You can also share mood charts or anxiety trackers—no fancy apps needed.

Keep it low-pressure. Some pairs prefer texting, some voice memos and others like the occasional coffee meetup. If you're not up for talking, it's fine to say; "Not up for chatting today, but I'm okay." Mutual respect and flexibility are most important.

Like any relationship, buddy systems have ups and downs. Life gets busy and sometimes one person pulls back. Talk openly about these moments—"If this ever gets to be too much, let's agree to pause or change things up." If your buddy stops responding, don't take it personally. People get distracted or overwhelmed for many reasons. Check in, but if there's no reply after some time, thank them for their support and consider finding someone new.

Rotating buddies can also prevent burnout. Some people switch buddies every few months, or keep multiple buddies for different types of support—one for daily texts, another for deeper talks. There's no set rule; the important thing is having at least one person you can be real with, even when things are tough.

It's normal for these partnerships to change over time as your needs or circumstances shift. Maybe you outgrow a buddy or want a break from regular check-ins—that's okay. You haven't failed; support is about what helps you, not meeting someone else's expectations.

Building and maintaining a check-in buddy system isn't always easy, but it pays off. Sharing both your wins and setbacks normalizes the highs and lows of anxiety management and you start to feel a part of a wider support web instead of stranded and alone. Even a single, honest message can break through a tough day.

As you finish this chapter, remember that support isn't about grand gestures or perfect words. It's about small, consistent acts of connection—one message, one call, one shared laugh at a time. In the next chapter, we'll explore how to spot anxiety triggers in your environment and shape routines that give you more peace, step by step.

Chapter 18

Handling Triggers—Mastering Your Environment

The Trigger Tracker—Spotting Patterns Before They Spiral

Have you ever found yourself tense and on edge, unsure of what set you off? Triggers rarely announce themselves—they slip quietly into your day and before you know it, you've gone from calm to frazzled. By the time you notice, you may already be caught in an anxious spiral.

That's where tracking helps. Consider the "Trigger Tracker" as a tool to observe and uncover clues about your anxiety—not to judge yourself, but to get curious. Tracking doesn't require a fancy system: A simple printable sheet, a journal page, or a phone notes app all work. Whenever anxiety flares, jot down the time, place, who's around, how your body feels and the thoughts rushing through your mind. Maybe it's 5pm in the kitchen alone, feeling restless and worrying; "I'll never get dinner ready on time." Or it's heart pounding and clammy hands in a crowded café. After a week of small notes, you'll often discover patterns that were hiding in plain sight.

Don't worry about perfection. Just be honest and gentle with yourself. It might feel awkward to pause and record your state in the moment. But after just a week, reviewing your notes often reveals recurring patterns: Certain times (like late afternoons), places, people, or sensations—like a tense jaw or fluttering stomach—show up repeatedly. Recording details makes invisible triggers visible.

After a week, review your entries for recurring themes. Are there particular locations, people, or social situations that consistently trigger anxiety? Does anxiety rise at specific times—like Mondays, after long meetings, or during transitions? Ask yourself: Which triggers can I influence? Maybe some (like social media checking or overbooking your schedule) are adjustable. Others are simply part of life for now—such as work meetings or family obligations?

Distinguishing avoidable from unavoidable triggers is empowering. Avoidable triggers are those you can change—certain apps, back-to-back commitments, or even foods that make you jittery. Unavoidable triggers are part of daily life: Required meetings, commutes, or caregiving. For avoidable triggers, experiment with boundaries—like unfollowing anxiety-inducing accounts or adding buffer time between tasks. For unavoidable ones, focus on self-compassion and coping strategies, such as playing calming music during tense commutes or practicing grounding breaths beforehand.

Remember, noticing patterns is progress in itself. Realizing triggers are real patterns—not just you "overreacting"—brings relief. Write down your "Top 3 Triggers" as a focus for your coping strategies. Keep them visible or saved in a note, so you can plan specific responses.

Interactive Element: Your Personalized Trigger Tracker

Take five minutes now to set up your weekly tracker. Draw three columns: Time/Place, People Present, Physical Sensations/Thoughts. Each time anxiety rises, jot a quick note—even just "3pm, living room, tight chest." At week's end, review and highlight any repeating patterns or surprises. Consider what you can change and what needs compassion. Awareness is your first win—change follows.

Real-Life Scenario Playbook—Scripts for Common Stressors

When anxiety hits in real life, you rarely get a heads-up or a chance to rehearse. You're in the thick of it—a meeting, a conversation, a traffic jam—and suddenly your nerves are on high alert. That's when having a ready-made script can change everything. Think of these as your emergency phrases and micro-actions, designed for those moments when you need a lifeline instead of a lecture.

Picture yourself mid-sentence at work and someone butts in before you've finished your thought. Your pulse jumps, frustration bubbles up and it's tempting to just let it go or shrink back. Instead, try this script: "Can I finish my thought and circle back to yours?" It's straightforward, calm and gives you back your voice without creating conflict. Or imagine facing a family member who starts in with criticism or prying questions. The old habits kick in—smile, nod, absorb—but this time you quietly say; "I'm not comfortable talking about that—can we change the subject?" Setting boundaries like this can feel risky the first few times, but with practice, your confidence grows. Now, let's say you're running late for something important—maybe a meeting or picking up your kid—and panic wants to take over. Instead of spiralling into self-blame or apologizing endlessly, breathe and remind yourself: "I'm doing my best to get there safely and that's enough." This tiny shift in self-talk can interrupt the storm of guilt and anxiety that so often follows.

Environmental cues and props make these scripts even more powerful. If you know you'll be walking into a high-stress situation, slip a grounding object into your pocket—a favourite ring, a smooth stone, even a dab of calming scent on your wrist. These aren't silly quirks;

they're anchors for your nervous system. During tense phone calls, you might discreetly squeeze a stress ball or run your thumb along a textured bracelet. It gives your brain something predictable to focus on when everything else feels out of control. Even something as simple as taking a slow sip of water creates space to pause before responding to a pointed question or comment.

Sometimes, triggers hit out of nowhere mid-day and you need to reset fast. For those moments, try this: Take one full breath in for two counts and exhale for four counts while counting ceiling tiles or watching light filter through blinds. If that doesn't cut it, do a five-second reality check—silently name one thing you see, one sound you hear and one sensation you feel (like your feet in your shoes or the chair under your legs). These micro-interventions send a message to your body that you're present and safe, breaking the anxious loop. Or get up if you can—stand tall, roll your shoulders back, stretch arms overhead. Even thirty seconds of movement can clear nervous energy when words alone won't help.

What works best is always personal. One person's script might feel awkward or forced to someone else. That's why you should experiment and customize these scenarios to fit your own life. Consider this prompt: "Write your own script for your #1 most frequent trigger." Maybe it's for saying no to extra work or telling a friend you need space. If you want more practice, role-play with a trusted check-in buddy or therapist—it builds muscle memory for real life. Remember: Preparedness isn't pessimism; it's self-empowerment. You aren't predicting disaster; you're giving yourself tools for any storm that comes your way.

The Sunday Prep Ritual—Reducing Weekday Anxiety

Sunday has a strange energy, doesn't it? For many anxious adults, Sunday afternoons can feel like the edge of a cliff—the week ahead looming, your mind already racing through tasks, worries and everything that might go sideways. That's why creating a Sunday ritual can be such a game-changer. Instead of letting the week sneak up on you, you take just a little bit of time to set yourself up so Monday (and all those days that follow) feel less like an ambush and more like a plan you actually had a say in.

Start simple. Pull out your calendar—digital or paper, whatever works. Glance at what's coming up. Are there meetings that always leave you wrung out? Kids' activities that have you scrambling? Appointments stacked too close together? Note anything that jumps out as likely to trigger stress. Now, prep what you can. Lay out outfits for a couple of days. Chop fruit and prep snacks—just enough to avoid that frantic hunt at 7am when everyone's hungry and nothing is ready. Set reminders on your phone for events you know will slip your mind in the chaos. If you have kids, check their backpacks, sign forms and make sure shoes actually have matches. Some people double-check their commute routes for surprises; others set up their work bag or charge devices overnight. The point isn't to do everything, but to do enough that Monday feels softer.

One step that makes a real difference is setting buffer zones in your schedule. After tough meetings or draining events, block out 10 to 15 minutes just for yourself—even if it's only to step outside, stretch, or scroll through something silly on your phone. These short pauses can be the difference between surviving your day and feeling like it's eating you alive. You can also sprinkle in mindful breaks between stacked commitments—a quick walk around the block, three deep breaths with your eyes closed at your desk, or even just sitting quietly with a cup of something warm. These little moments help your brain reset instead of letting stress pile up without relief.

But don't stop at prepping for stress—actively build in anchor points to look forward to. Plan for one small treat or moment of joy each day. Maybe it's coffee with a friend on Tuesday, listening to a favourite podcast while folding laundry, or saving your go-to TV show for Thursday night when you know the week will be wearing thin. If you like movement, book a midweek yoga or fitness class—something that feels like a reward, not another obligation. Tiny bright spots scattered through the week act as lifelines, reminding you there's more ahead than just ticking boxes.

At the end of the week, take five minutes to review and tweak your routine. What smoothed things out? Which bits felt unnecessary or caused more stress than they saved? Jot down quick notes—keep what helps, change what doesn't. If you live with family or roommates, share this ritual together so everyone knows what's happening and can support each other. Some readers even check in with friends or accountability buddies: "Did you do your Sunday prep?" That sense of camaraderie makes it easier to stick with new habits.

A reader once told me, "Sunday prep made my whole week feel less like a surprise attack." That stuck with me because it sums up what these rituals offer—a sense of control where anxiety used to run the show. You won't get rid of every stressor, but you'll meet them on steadier ground.

As you wrap up this chapter, remember that shaping your environment is about more than managing triggers; it's about building pockets of calm and hope into the everyday grind. Up next: How to track progress and celebrate small wins as you keep moving forward.

Chapter 19

Progress You Can See—Tracking, Celebrating, and Adjusting

Anxiety Check-In Logs—Making the Invisible Visible

Anxiety often feels elusive, shifting like a shadow. We notice big spikes—a panic attack before a meeting, a wave of worry late at night—but smaller patterns slip by. Living with anxiety is like tracking unpredictable weather and you're supposed to predict it. An anxiety check-in log makes the invisible tangible—a real account of highs, lows and overlooked in-between moments.

Here's why it matters: When anxiety is high, your mind tries to convince you that you're stuck or getting worse. But a check-in log—whether in a bullet journal, in a mood tracker app, or on a printed template—reveals trends and triggers your memory would easily miss. Maybe Mondays are always tense, or you notice your symptoms ease up after moving your body at lunch. These aren't just random notes—they're valuable clues. Over time, your log becomes a map of what triggers you, what soothes you and what counts as progress, even when it's subtle. Many apps come with customizable prompts, reminders and color-coded mood charts, making it simple to start (Best Mood Tracker Apps, source 1).

A sample log might be:

DATE	SETTING	SYMPTOMS	COPING TOOLS USED	OUTCOME
7/4	Work Meeting	Heart racing, Dizzy	Box breathing	Felt steadier after 3 minutes
7/6	Home, Evening	Restless, Irritable	Journalling	Calmed enough to sleep
7/8	Grocery Store	Stomach Knots	Drinking water, Grounding	Anxiety dropped by half

Don't feel pressured to fill every section or record every day. This tool is for you, not a performance—honesty is the priority. Don't just log tough days; good days matter too. Use prompts like: "What patterns am I seeing? What's changing?" One reader put it simply: "Logging helped me see I was actually improving, even if I didn't always feel like I was." Sometimes, you spot yourself using more tools, rebounding quicker, or just having fewer intense days.

To keep the habit going, pair it with something you already do—scribble a few lines with your morning coffee, add quick notes at lunch, or check in before bed as part of your nightly routine. Set gentle reminders if needed. Keeping it simple and routine helps it stick—without making it another source of stress.

Logs also become invaluable in conversations with therapists, doctors, or support people. Instead of relying on memory, you can bring up your notes or a printed log and share specific patterns from the past weeks. This is especially helpful if you're changing medications or trying new coping strategies—did your sleep change? Are panic attacks less frequent? Sharing your insights with a support buddy, friend, or family member can foster understanding and let others see your real experience.

Try It Yourself: Anxiety Check-In Log Template

Exercise: Copy this table into your journal or app for a week. Each morning or evening, record:

- Date
- Where anxiety showed up (setting)
- Physical/emotional symptoms
- Coping tool(s) you used (or wish you had)
- What happened after (outcome)

After a week, reflect: Are triggers recurring? Did any tool surprise you? Was there an unexpectedly good day? Stay gentle and curious—this log is for growth, not self-criticism.

Celebrating Small Wins – Turning Progress into Motivation

Success for most anxious adults is subtle, gradual and rarely dramatic. Change often appears in minor ways—managing a tough morning better than before, pausing before reacting, or reaching out for help, even if it feels awkward. Spotting and celebrating these small victories is a powerful motivator for managing anxiety long-term. Recognizing your smallest improvements—like breathing deeply before spiralling or sending a difficult text—shifts your self-talk from "I'm stuck" to "I'm moving forward." You don't need to wait for big milestones; every gain builds hope and confidence, making future progress easier. Though easy to dismiss, these tiny steps are the foundation of lasting change (Why Celebrating Small Wins Matters).

Celebration doesn't need to be flashy or public. Choose what feels genuine to you. Some people enjoy a quick dance break, noting a win in a journal, or texting a friend: "Guess what I managed today?" Having someone to share with can strengthen your sense of achievement. Others prefer physical rituals, like adding a marble to a jar, a sticker to the calendar, or a post it on a "win wall." If you'd rather keep it private, a whispered "good job" or a hand squeeze is enough. The key is that your celebration matches your personality.

Making Celebration a Habit

Pair your celebration with regular check-ins to maximize its effect. Recording both struggles and wins helps you notice resilience, not just setbacks. Maybe you went out for five minutes instead of staying in, or reached out for support when you wanted to hide—those count. Routinely celebrating, such as during a nightly reflection or a weekly "win review," builds the habit. One reader shared, "Celebrating the little things made me want to keep trying new tools. I started looking for chances to succeed instead of waiting for proof I was failing." This shift fuels hope and encourages trying new strategies.

Finding Wins Everywhere

Look for wins in less obvious places. Sending a dreaded email, pausing before reacting, or breathing mindfully instead of scrolling endlessly are all accomplishments. Wins aren't just about reducing symptoms; sometimes they're about self-kindness during setbacks rather than self-criticism. Consider these celebration ideas: Treat yourself, share your win in a group, take a short walk, play a favourite song, journal about success, give yourself a high five, or quietly acknowledge your progress.

Keeping a Record

On hard days, your collection of wins—via a notebook, marble jar, or digital log—becomes a vital reminder that progress is real. Reviewing your track record helps challenge anxiety's narrative of being stuck. Even glancing at your wins monthly can reinvigorate motivation when it wanes. Over time, these celebrations build self-trust and resilience, helping you keep going, even when anxiety says otherwise.

When to Adjust Your Toolbox—Signs It's Time for a Change

Managing anxiety is not about finding one perfect tool and sticking with it forever. Our needs shift. Life throws curveballs. What used to help you feel grounded might suddenly seem flat or even annoying. Maybe you notice routines that once brought relief now just feel like chores, or you catch yourself skipping over a tool because it doesn't bring comfort anymore. Sometimes, you might sense that setbacks are happening more often, or the old strategies aren't enough for your current stress. Big life changes—like a new job, moving, or parenting challenges—can also make old tools less effective. I remember a time when my grounding exercise, which had been my favourite for months, started feeling mechanical and hollow. I realized I was going through the motions and needed something fresh. That's not a setback; it's a sign of growth.

Recognizing when it's time to adjust isn't always obvious. Look for clues like boredom, growing dread around routines, or increased anxiety despite regular practice. If you notice you're avoiding a tool, that's feedback, not failure. Think of it as outgrowing shoes—they served you well, but now something else fits better. Here's a quick chart to help clarify:

Old Tool - New Need.

- Journaling (now stale) - Try voice memos instead.
- Breathing app (boredom) - Add a walking meditation.
- Reading affirmations - Switch to music cues.
- Counting breaths - Experiment with yoga.
- Static routine - Create a seasonal ritual

Updating your toolbox doesn't have to be overwhelming. Start by reviewing your recent logs or win trackers for patterns. Notice which tools you reach for automatically versus the ones you skip or dread.

Ask yourself honestly: Which strategies make me feel energized or soothed? Which do I only do out of habit? Once you spot the stale or ineffective ones, brainstorm something new to try this week—a different sensory grounding, a movement-based reset, or even a playful ritual with your kids. Research options online or trade ideas with a friend.

Shifting your toolbox is not regression; it's evidence that you're adapting and paying attention to what you need right now. Growth means leaving behind what no longer serves you and making space for new possibilities. I once clung to a particular journaling method long after it stopped working because I felt loyal to my old routine. Letting it go made room for voice notes, which brought back a sense of relief and even fun. Changing your approach means you're listening to yourself and respecting your current reality.

Stay curious about what works and what doesn't. Your best tools will change as you do and that's healthy. Try setting a reminder every few months—at the start of each season—to revisit your toolbox. Ask yourself: What feels inspiring right now? Is there something I'm itching to try—a summer routine that gets you outside, or a winter comfort activity for cozy nights? Sometimes trading ideas with a check-in buddy can spark new strategies neither of you would have found alone.

Adjusting your anxiety toolkit keeps your approach fresh and relevant to your real life. The goal is not perfection—it's responsiveness and honesty with yourself as your needs change. This chapter's main lesson is simple: What works today might not work tomorrow and that's okay. By checking in with your tools and updating them as needed, you stay flexible and empowered on your path toward more peace.

Next up, we'll turn toward building community and finding support beyond yourself—because managing anxiety is easier when you don't do it all alone.

Chapter 20

Community, Compassion, and Your Next Step

Joining the Conversation—Finding Your Safe Community

Feeling alone in your struggles is common, but finding even one person who relates can make a huge difference. Community doesn't cure anxiety, but it provides a space to breathe, share burdens and realize you're less alone than you think.

Supportive communities exist in many forms: Online forums allow you to participate at your own pace, private groups offer smaller, moderated spaces and peer circles focus on shared experiences and practical support. Book clubs and local meetups provide structure and accountability. The most helpful spaces are nonjudgmental, inclusive and value confidentiality. Prioritize groups with gentle advice, mutual respect and supportive guidance, not competitive conversations.

If diving in feels daunting, start as an observer—read others' posts and learn how the group operates. When you're ready, a simple introduction works: "Hi, I'm new here and just getting comfortable. I struggle with anxious thoughts and wanted to see if anyone else has tips for handling stressful mornings?" Or simply state, "I'm here to learn—I appreciate this space." Move at your own pace; you choose when to participate more.

Interactive Element: Reflection Prompt

Write down what a "safe community" means to you. What qualities are most important—confidentiality, empathy, shared wisdom? Where would you look for support—a parent group, online forum, local class? Draft a one-sentence introduction you'd feel comfortable posting when ready.

The "Not for Everyone" List—Letting Go of What Doesn't Work

Not every tool, tip, or community will suit you. Sometimes widely recommended practices like a meditation app, deep breathing, gratitude journaling, or a certain support group just don't resonate. You might give them a fair try and still feel more restless or discouraged. This doesn't mean you're doing it wrong or something is wrong with you. Recognizing what isn't helpful—and letting it go—is a quiet wisdom, a sign of tuning into what you uniquely need.

Make your own "Not for Me" list. Instead of forcing something that drains you, write it down and give yourself permission to move on. When to let go? Notice how you feel: Persistent dread, frustration, or boredom—even after trying to adjust. If your anxiety grows, or you feel resentful rather than relieved, that's a sign. Ask yourself: "Does this leave me steadier or more frazzled?" If it tips toward frazzled, try tweaking the details—like time, place, or the way you do it. If it still doesn't work, let it go. Real progress means listening to your own signals and respecting them.

Quick Exercise: Try-Tweak-Toss Flowchart

Draw three circles labelled Try → Tweak → Toss. When a strategy fizzles, start at "Try." If it doesn't work, adjust at "Tweak." Still flopping? Move to "Toss." This isn't giving up—it's making room for what truly helps.

Your Personalized Coping Toolbox—A Living Document

Your coping toolbox shouldn't collect dust on a shelf or get buried in phone notes you never open. It works best as a living, breathing resource—something you reach for when life gets bumpy, but also something you check in with during the quieter days. Think of it as your personal anxiety "first aid kit," but with room to grow and change as your seasons of life shift. You might love grounding exercises in winter, then lean into movement or outdoor rituals when the sun returns. Set aside time every quarter—or with the changing seasons—to review and update what's working and what's not. This doesn't have to be formal; sometimes a cup of coffee and a few sticky notes are all you need. Keep your toolbox visible: Tape a checklist inside a closet door, snap a photo and make it your phone background, or jot a quick "top five" on your bathroom mirror. Use this simple audit template: What's helping? What feels stale or forced? What would you like to try next? Celebrate new tools, even the tiny ones, by adding a sticker to your calendar, texting a friend, or lighting a candle to mark the occasion. Your needs will change—so let your toolbox change with you, always reflecting who you are right now, not who you think you should be.

The Compassion Contract—A Promise to Yourself

Sometimes you need more than a list of coping strategies or reminders from friends. You need something solid—a real promise to yourself that you'll offer understanding, not punishment, when anxiety gets loud or progress feels slow. That's where a compassion contract comes in. It's a simple, intentional agreement to treat yourself with the same kindness you offer others. This isn't about being soft or letting yourself off the hook. It's about giving yourself space to breathe, especially when you slip up or stumble. Self-commitment can be surprisingly powerful. Writing down your intention or saying it out loud creates a small anchor, something you can return to when your inner critic tries to take over. Fill in the blanks with your own language: "I promise to treat myself with patience when I feel overwhelmed. I will pause and breathe before judging myself harshly. When I fall short, I will remind myself I am learning, not failing." You can sign this contract with a favourite pen, tuck it in your wallet, or even recite it in the shower. Some find it meaningful to read it with a trusted friend, therapist, or partner as witness. As life shifts, revisit your words—maybe every month, maybe just when things feel shaky. Adjust them to fit your current reality. The contract is yours alone: Flexible, private and always open to edits when you need more grace or a gentle nudge forward.

Digital Resources—Worksheets, Trackers, and Guided Scripts

Managing anxiety can feel overwhelming, especially when stressful moments pop up without warning. That's why having digital support on hand matters more than ever. You don't need to remember every grounding exercise, self-compassion phrase, or progress chart—sometimes, you just need them accessible on your phone or laptop. Inside your digital toolkit, you'll find anxiety trackers designed to help you spot patterns and triggers over time, grounding exercise scripts that walk you through calming steps in plain language and progress charts to visualize your small wins. There are also self-compassion worksheets with fill-in-the-blank prompts, so you can practice talking to yourself like you would a friend. Download these as PDFs or keep them in your favourite notes app for quick access. You might find that checking off a tracker or reading a script out loud brings a sense of structure when everything else feels scattered. Try setting a reminder to fill out your mood chart before bed, or use a grounding script as part of your pre-meeting ritual. Sharing these resources with a friend, therapist, or check-in buddy can help make the process less lonely—and sometimes, swapping tips leads to new insights. Adapt these tools as you go: Use what clicks, skip what doesn't. Digital support isn't about perfection; it's about having help right when you need it most.

Reader Stories—Real Voices, Real Hope

When you hear about anxiety, it often feels faceless—just symptoms and definitions. But real people live with it every day, in ways that are messy, surprising and sometimes beautifully ordinary. Take Jess, a mother of two in her late thirties who used to dread school pickup. She once sat in her car, palms sweaty, rehearsing what she might say if another parent approached. Now, she keeps a small stone in her pocket, rubbing it gently when nerves spike. She says the stone doesn't fix her worries, but it gives her a moment of calm—a tiny win that makes the chaos quieter.

Or picture Malik, a grad student who always seemed pulled together on paper but struggled with panic attacks before presentations. After one disastrous seminar, he wrote a note to himself: "You survived before; you'll survive again." He reads it before every big moment now and while his anxiety hasn't disappeared, he isn't frozen anymore. Then there's Rosa, recently retired, who found relief just by naming her anxiety aloud to her partner for the first time at sixty-one. Her world didn't end. Instead, she felt lighter.

These stories aren't about perfection or dramatic transformations. They're about small moments of resilience—finding hope on tough days or sharing a laugh after a setback. If you ever feel brave enough, your story might help someone else breathe easier too. Sometimes hearing, "me too," is the most comforting thing of all.

Your Next Small Step—What to Try Today

Progress doesn't require grand gestures. Your next step can be as simple as a breath, jotting a note in your phone, or pausing before you respond to a text. You could stand in sunlight for a minute before checking your messages, write down a single worry and set it aside, or skip scrolling social media before bed. Giving yourself permission to say, "I'm at capacity right now," is a valid win. When things feel heavy, even just acknowledging your feelings is meaningful progress.

Consider what's possible for you today. You might try a short grounding exercise, list three small positives, or drink your coffee without multitasking. Maybe a quick check-in with a friend or reading a supportive quote helps. For some, a momentary retreat—closing your eyes and letting the world spin on without you—is what's needed. There's no one right starting point; it's about what offers support in this moment.

Every action, however minor, is a win. You don't need to take on everything at once—progress happens in small, genuine steps. Today, value whatever you can do, even if it's as simple as showing yourself kindness when your inner critic is loud. One small step is always enough.

This wraps up your toolkit for living with anxiety. Each choice to care for yourself matters, building momentum for whatever comes next.

Conclusion

If you've made it here, I want you to take a deep breath and really let that land. You showed up for yourself, page after page, even when anxiety tried to convince you that you couldn't. That's no small thing. It's the opposite of small—it's brave and it's real.

Let's step back for a moment. Remember where we began? Maybe it was 2am, staring at the ceiling, your mind spinning with what-ifs. Or maybe it was in the middle of a crowded grocery store, heart pounding, wishing you could just disappear. Maybe it was after a work meeting where you held yourself together on the outside but felt like you were falling apart inside. Wherever you started, you probably felt alone, overwhelmed and maybe even a little hopeless.

But turning these pages, you started building something different. You mapped your own anxiety landscape—not someone else's version. You named your real triggers, from the tiniest micro-stressors to the big, loud moments. You learned to spot early warning signs and to pause instead of powering through. You found ways to ground yourself, whether in the cereal aisle, the car at school pickup, or during a tense meeting. You built your own toolbox—one that fits your actual life, not an idealized one.

And you did it all with a spirit of self-compassion, even if that felt awkward or new. You reminded yourself, maybe for the first time, that progress matters more than perfection. That you don't have to be anxiety-free to be okay or worthy. That you're not broken, just human.

Throughout this book, we've circled back to that core message again and again: You are not alone in your struggle. Anxiety is not a personal flaw or a sign you're doing life wrong. It's something your brain and body do to try to keep you safe—just a little too enthusiastically sometimes. You've learned to notice your patterns, to gently interrupt spirals and to respond with curiosity instead of criticism. That's powerful.

You've picked up real-life tools along the way. You know how to anchor yourself with your senses, how to calm racing thoughts with a bedtime "worry dump" and how to use tiny rituals to reset during the day. You've learned scripts for setting boundaries and saying no, for surviving panic in public and for handling social situations that used to make you freeze. You even practiced what to do when tools don't work—how to adapt, toss, or swap them without shame. You built a personalized coping toolbox and learned to update it as your life changes.

You learned that setbacks are part of the deal. Bad days will happen. Tools will feel stale sometimes. The old self-critical voice will sneak in. But now, you know that a tough day doesn't erase your progress. It's just a signal to pause, reset and try again. Every time you reach for a tool, even if it's just one breath or a quick pause, you're proving to yourself that you can do hard things.

I want to pause here and celebrate you. It takes real courage to face anxiety head-on. It takes even more courage to try new things, to experiment, to fail and try again. Every small win you tracked, every moment you chose self-kindness, every time you let yourself rest or reached out for help—those are victories. Don't let anyone, especially your inner critic, tell you otherwise.

You now have a library of tools for daily relief, a set of flexible routines for ongoing change and scripts for real-life moments when anxiety shows up unannounced. You have permission to adapt these tools, to let go of what doesn't work and to try something new whenever you need. That's resilience in action.

As you close this book, I hope you'll keep offering yourself self-kindness. When anxiety resurfaces (and it will), remember: You are not starting over. You're continuing the journey. One tool. One breath. One boundary. That's how progress is built. You're not failing if you need a reset. You're human. That's a win.

Don't forget that support matters. Lean on your people—your check-in buddy, your partner, your trusted friends. Join safe communities, whether online or in person. And if you ever need more help, reaching out to a professional isn't failure—it's wisdom and strength. Let yourself be supported. You're allowed.

Your toolbox isn't a museum piece. It's a living, breathing resource. Look at it often. Refresh it as your needs change. Celebrate every new tool you add, every step you take, every small win you notice. Keep your wins visible, even if that means a sticker on your calendar or a happy dance in your kitchen.

So, what now? Take one small step. Maybe it's trying a grounding ritual you haven't used yet. Maybe it's texting a friend or joining a group. Maybe it's sitting in the sun for two minutes or practicing your evening check-out. One step is enough. You don't have to do it all. Just keep moving, gently, in your own way.

I believe in your ability to reclaim your inner peace, not because you'll never feel anxious again, but because you now have the tools, self-awareness and courage to meet anxiety as it comes. You're equipped. You're resilient. You're worthy of support, rest and compassion.

Thank you for letting me walk this part of the journey with you. Remember: You're not alone, you're not broken and every single small step forward matters. Your story isn't about anxiety—it's about strength, hope and building a life that feels lighter, one manageable action at a time. Keep going. I'm cheering you on, every step of the way.

References

American Psychological Association. (n.d.). *How do I find a good therapist?* https://www.apa.org/ptsd-guideline/patients-and-families/finding-good-therapist

Anxiety and Depression Association of America. (n.d.). *Spouse or partner.* https://adaa.org/finding-help/helping-others/spouse-or-partner

Anxiety Care UK. (n.d.). *Setbacks.* https://anxietycare.org.uk/setbacks/

Ahead App. (2025, January 17). *The science of morning routines: How your brain benefits from strategic self-care.* https://ahead-app.com/blog/procrastination/the-science-of-morning-routines-how-your-brain-benefits-from-strategic-self-care-20250117-033255

Be Ceremonial. (n.d.). *6 rituals that can help manage stress.* https://www.beceremonial.com/blog/6-rituals-that-can-help-manage-stress/

Better Place Health. (n.d.). *5 micro-interventions for anxiety that take less than 60 seconds.* https://betterplacehealth.com/5-micro-interventions-for-anxiety-that-take-less-than-60-seconds/

Beyond Blue. (n.d.). *10 strategies for managing anxiety.* https://www.beyondblue.org.au/mental-health/anxiety/treatments-for-anxiety/anxiety-management-strategies

BrainFacts.org. (2018, June 29). *What part of the brain deals with anxiety? What can brains affected by anxiety tell us?* https://www.brainfacts.org/diseases-and-disorders/mental-health/2018/what-part-of-the-brain-deals-with-anxiety-what-can-brains-affected-by-anxiety-tell-us-062918

Brown University Health. (n.d.). *Children, anxiety and tips for parents.* https://www.brownhealth.org/be-well/children-anxiety-and-tips-parents

Cabeen, J. (n.d.). *The 5-minute brain dump: A simple strategy for clarity and focus.* https://jessicacabeen.com/the-5-minute-brain-dump-a-simple-strategy-for-clarity-and-focus/

CapC. (n.d.). *Checking in with your buddy.* https://www.capc.org/documents/download/1054/

Choosing Therapy. (2025). *Best journal app of 2025: Our firsthand experiences.* https://www.choosingtherapy.com/best-journal-apps/

CNBC. (2023, October 11). *Harvard-trained psychologist: 60-second exercise to fight work stress.* https://www.cnbc.com/2023/10/11/harvard-trained-psychologist-60-second-exercise-to-fight-work-stress.html

Cleveland Clinic. (n.d.). *Amygdala: What it is and what it controls.* https://my.clevelandclinic.org/health/body/24894-amygdala

Cleveland Clinic. (n.d.). *How box breathing can help you destress.* https://health.clevelandclinic.org/box-breathing-benefits

Cohesive Therapy NYC. (n.d.). *5 discreet exercises to calm anxiety in public.*

https://cohesivetherapynyc.com/blog/5-discreet-exercises-to-calm-anxiety-in-public/

Cornell Health. (n.d.). *Anxiety tracking log*. https://health.cornell.edu/sites/health/files/pdf-library/anxiety-tracking-log.pdf

Earthing Harmony. (n.d.). *54321 grounding: A science-backed mindfulness technique for calm and connection*. https://earthingharmony.com/blogs/general/54321-grounding-a-science-backed-mindfulness-technique-for-calm-and-connection

Every Mind Matters (NHS). (n.d.). *Reframing unhelpful thoughts*. https://www.nhs.uk/every-mind-matters/mental-wellbeing-tips/self-help-cbt-techniques/reframing-unhelpful-thoughts/

GoodRx. (n.d.). *7 telltale signs you may need help for your anxiety*. https://www.goodrx.com/health-topic/anxiety-disorders/when-to-seek-help-for-anxiety

Healthline. (n.d.). *11 common anxiety triggers and how to identify yours*. https://www.healthline.com/health/anxiety/anxiety-triggers

Healthline. (n.d.). *Box breathing: How to, benefits, and tips*. https://www.healthline.com/health/copd/box-breathing

Healthline. (n.d.). *30 grounding techniques to quiet distressing thoughts*. https://www.healthline.com/health/grounding-techniques

Healthline. (n.d.). *5 tips for safely navigating panic attacks in public*. https://www.healthline.com/health/mental-health/panic-attacks-in-public

Healthline. (n.d.). *Cognitive distortions: 10 examples of distorted thinking*. https://www.healthline.com/health/cognitive-distortions

Hopkins Medicine. (n.d.). *How to help someone with anxiety*. https://www.hopkinsmedicine.org/health/treatment-tests-and-therapies/how-to-help-someone-with-anxiety

Indeed. (n.d.). *How to nicely say "no" (with 50 examples)*. https://www.indeed.com/career-advice/career-development/how-to-nicely-say-no

Insight Timer. (n.d.). *Alternatives to meditation: 14 techniques that work*. https://insighttimer.com/blog/alternatives-to-meditation/

Jed Foundation. (n.d.). *How to build an anxiety toolkit*. https://jedfoundation.org/resource/how-to-build-an-anxiety-toolkit/

Medical News Today. (n.d.). *Fight, flight, or freeze response: Signs, causes, and recovery*. https://www.medicalnewstoday.com/articles/fight-flight-or-freeze-response

Mental Health America. (n.d.). *Building your coping toolbox*. https://mhanational.org/resources/building-your-coping-toolbox/

Mental Health Center Kids. (n.d.). *100 positive affirmations for anxiety relief*. https://mentalhealthcenterkids.com/blogs/articles/positive-affirmations-for-anxiety

Mind Soother Therapy. (n.d.). *Try these grounding techniques*. https://www.mindsoother.com/blog/grounding-techniques-to-practice-when-youre-anxious-in-public

MSU Extension. (n.d.). *Explaining your anxiety or depression to your child*. https://www.canr.msu.edu/news/explaining_your_anxiety_or_depression_to_your_child

Mayo Clinic. (n.d.). *Fear of public speaking: How can I overcome it?* https://www.mayoclinic.org/diseases-conditions/specific-phobias/expert-answers/fear-of-public-speaking/faq-20058416

National Sleep Foundation. (n.d.). *Cognitive behavioural therapy for insomnia (CBT-I): An overview.* https://www.sleepfoundation.org/insomnia/treatment/cognitive-behavioral-therapy-insomnia

National Sleep Foundation. (n.d.). *How to build a better bedtime routine for adults.* https://www.sleepfoundation.org/sleep-hygiene/bedtime-routine-for-adults

National Sleep Foundation. (n.d.). *Anxiety at night: Causes and tips for relief.* https://www.sleepfoundation.org/mental-health/anxiety-at-night

Positive Psychology. (n.d.). *7 best mood trackers to chart and journal your feelings.* https://positivepsychology.com/mood-charts-track-your-mood/

Positive Psychology. (n.d.). *8 powerful self-compassion exercises & worksheets (+PDF).* https://positivepsychology.com/self-compassion-exercises-worksheets/

Positive Psychology. (n.d.). *Living with the inner critic: 8 helpful worksheets (+PDF).* https://positivepsychology.com/inner-critic-worksheets/

Positive Psychology. (n.d.). *How to practice self-compassion: 8 techniques and tips.* https://positivepsychology.com/how-to-practice-self-compassion/

Positive Psychology. (n.d.). *Role play in therapy: 21 scripts & examples.* https://positivepsychology.com/role-playing-scripts/

PsychCentral. (n.d.). *The psychology behind people pleasing.* https://psychcentral.com/health/the-need-to-please-the-psychology-of-people-pleasing

PsychCentral. (n.d.). *5 ways to practice self-compassion for anxiety.* https://psychcentral.com/anxiety/5-ways-to-practice-self-compassion-for-anxiety

Psychology Today. (2023, June). *Is decision overload affecting your mental health?* https://www.psychologytoday.com/us/blog/high-octane-women/202306/is-decision-overload-affecting-your-mental-health

Psychology Today. (2024, June). *6 common fears about starting therapy.* https://www.psychologytoday.com/ie/blog/the-psychology-of-relationships-and-emotional-intelligence/202406/6-common-fears-about

Raising Children Network. (n.d.). *Self-compassion for parents.* https://raisingchildren.net.au/grown-ups/looking-after-yourself/wellbeing/self-compassion-for-parents

SAMHSA. (n.d.). *Free & low cost treatment options for mental health and substance use.* https://www.samhsa.gov/find-support/how-to-pay-for-treatment/free-or-low-cost-treatment

Self-Compassion.org. (n.d.). *Self-compassion practices: Cultivate inner peace and joy.* https://self-compassion.org/self-compassion-practices/

Sleep Foundation. (n.d.). *Journaling prompts for better sleep.* https://organizations.headspace.com/blog/brain-dump-for-a-good-nights-sleep

Summer @ Harvard. (n.d.). *Why celebrating small wins matters.* https://summer.harvard.edu/blog/why-celebrating-small-wins-matters/

The Everygirl. (n.d.). *15 Sunday rituals to set you up for an amazing week.* https://theeverygirl.com/sunday-rituals/

The Skimm. (n.d.). *20 conversation starters for those with social anxiety.*

https://www.theskimm.com/skimm-scripts/conversation-starters-social-anxiety-script

Therapist Aid. (n.d.). *Communication worksheets.* https://www.therapistaid.com/therapy-worksheets/communication/none

Therapist Aid. (n.d.). *Anxiety worksheets.* https://www.therapistaid.com/therapy-worksheets/anxiety/none

Therapy Utah. (n.d.). *How setting boundaries can help anxiety.* https://www.therapyutah.org/how-setting-boundaries-can-help-anxiety/

Verywell Mind. (n.d.). *How to create your own 'safe space' for when you feel overwhelmed.* https://www.verywellmind.com/how-and-why-you-should-create-a-safe-space-for-yourself-3144981

Verywell Mind. (n.d.). *The characteristics of high-functioning anxiety.* https://www.verywellmind.com/what-is-high-functioning-anxiety-4140198

Verywell Mind. (2024). *Best online anxiety support groups of 2024.* https://www.verywellmind.com/best-online-anxiety-support-groups-4692353

Verywell Mind. (n.d.). *Best mood tracker apps.* https://www.verywellmind.com/best-mood-tracker-apps-5212922

Weber State University. (n.d.). *Creating digital boundaries: Having a strategy for managing screen time.* https://www.weber.edu/academicpeercoaching/blog/digital-boundaries.html

Zencare. (n.d.). *Habit stacking for mental health: The ultimate guide.* https://blog.zencare.co/habit-stacking-for-mental-health/

www.ingramcontent.com/pod-product-compliance
Lightning Source LLC
Chambersburg PA
CBHW061728070526
44583CB00024B/3058